100

THINGS TO DO IN
DETROIT
BEFORE YOU
DIE

100

THINGS TO DO IN
DETROIT
BEFORE YOU
DIE

· ·

AMY S. ECKERT

REEDY PRESS

Library of Congress Control Number: 2015957547

ISBN: 9781681060323

Design by Jill Halpin

All Images: Amy S. Eckert

Printed in the United States of America
16 17 18 19 20   5 4 3 2 1

Please note that websites, phone numbers, addresses, and company names are subject to change or cancellation. We did our best to relay the most accurate information available, but due to circumstances beyond our control, please do not hold us liable for misinformation. When exploring new destinations, please do your homework before you go.

DEDICATION

To Betty and Charles Wibert, who made me a Detroiter.

● ●

CONTENTS

• •

PREFACE

The hardest part about writing *100 Things to Do in Detroit Before You Die* was limiting myself to one hundred. It seemed I no more whittled my list to one hundred when some great new attraction would open . . . leaving me second-guessing myself.

Detroit is a city on the rise. Once abandoned buildings have morphed into trendy boutiques. Once desolate city blocks buzz with chef-owned restaurant districts. And since it turns out that no one is more fiercely supportive of Detroit than Detroiters, you can be sure that the vast majority of these new shops and restaurants are independently owned, one-of-a-kind, nowhere-else-but-in-Detroit kinds of places. Whether you've loved Detroit all your life or are just now giving the city a chance, the transformation is exhilarating. And it's ongoing.

Of course, Detroit offers plenty of timeless favorites, can't-miss stops that ought to sit on any visitor's radar. I've included those sites in this book: the Motown Museum, where a generation's musical mainstays were born; the Henry Ford Museum, a treasure trove of Americana; and the Detroit Institute of Arts, repository of the finest Diego Rivera you are likely ever to see.

Add to the list Detroit's up-and-coming attractions and you can quickly fill a weekend with Motor City fun: Gold Cash Gold, a former pawn shop turned trendy restaurant in Corktown; Selden Standard, a vegetarian- and vegan-friendly Midtown eatery supplied

• •

at least in part by Detroit's urban gardens; and the assembly line tour at one of America's most popular luxury watchmakers, Shinola.

Consider this list of one hundred a starting point, then, the one hundred things that this Detroit-lover thinks you should not miss while in The D. Whether you've lived in Detroit all your life or are just now becoming curious about Michigan's largest city, you'll find plenty of things old and new to discover. And chances are, you'll find a few new gems, too. Detroit is a city whose list just keeps on growing.

Welcome to Detroit!

—Amy S. Eckert

ACKNOWLEDGMENTS

A big thank you to Renee Monforton, Deanna Majchrzak, and the entire staff of the Detroit Metro Convention & Visitors Bureau. Every question I have, you answer. Every new Detroit attraction that opens, you make sure I know about it. I couldn't do what I do without you.

FOOD AND DRINK

DISCOVER CREATIVE MENUS
IN CORKTOWN

In an up-and-coming city it's hard to find a more up-and-coming neighborhood than Detroit's Corktown, particularly when it comes to dining. The city's oldest surviving neighborhood was first settled by Irish immigrants from County Cork. But Corktown really got its boost in the latter half of the twentieth century when the Detroit Tigers's stadium drew a fan base large enough to support numerous restaurants, bars, and shops. Once the stadium moved downtown, the neighborhood fell into serious disrepair. These days Corktown ranks as one of the busiest of Detroit's resurging communities, largely thanks to a boom in independent, locally owned restaurants and bars. Look for gourmet burger and BBQ joints, artisanal coffeehouses and industrial-chic restaurants, all of them obsessive about using wholesome, locally sourced ingredients in creative ways.

Bobcat Bonnie's
1800 Michigan Ave., Detroit 48216
313-962-1383
bobcatbonnies.com

Gold Cash Gold
2100 Michigan Ave., Detroit 48216
313-242-0770
goldcashgolddetroit.com

Green Dot Stables
2200 W. Lafayette St., Detroit 48216
313-962-5588
greendotstables.com

Mercury Burger & Bar
2163 Michigan Ave., Detroit 48216
313-964-5000
mercuryburgerbar.com

Ottava Via
1400 Michigan Ave., Detroit 48216
313-962-5500
facebook.com/ottava.via

Slows Bar BQ
2138 Michigan Ave., Detroit 48216
313-962-9828
slowsbarbq.com

LOAD UP
ON LOCAL PRODUCE
AT EASTERN MARKET

Since 1841 Detroiters have been buying their produce and cut flowers at Eastern Market, making this one of the oldest markets in the United States. Six sheds sprawl across four and a half acres and several city blocks near the heart of downtown, each sheltering stands loaded with fresh meat and fish, honey, preserves, and baked goods as well as fresh fruits and veggies, some of it grown in urban gardens that have sprung up where Detroit's abandoned buildings once stood. The Saturday Market is held year-round with additional market days in the warm weather months. Not in town on market day? You can find plenty of small produce shops, butchers, bakeries, and the like open in this neighborhood every day of the week, even at times the larger market isn't.

2934 Russell St., Detroit 48207
easternmarket.com

TIP
Parking is free at the Eastern Market Garage on Riopelle Street except on tailgating Sundays. If the garage is full, head to the south parking lot at Russell Street and the Fisher Freeway.

SIP A COLD ONE
AT DETROIT'S CRAFT BREWERIES

Detroit is a blue-collar city through and through, and as such, a beer-drinking city. The last of its large, traditional brewers, Stroh's, left in 1985, creating something of a drought in locally brewed suds. But when craft brewing began to pick up, Detroit jumped on the bandwagon early. The largest city in a state that ranks among the nation's top ten in beer production, Detroit's brewers produce a wide variety of beers, including lagers and ales, meads, sour beers, and Belgians. Most of the city's restaurants and bars support Detroit and Michigan craft brewers by reserving their taps for local beers. But you'll find the brewers' best selection at the tasting rooms themselves. Scattered from downtown to the outer suburbs, from the edges of the Cultural District to the working class neighborhoods, the Motor City brims with microbreweries.

Atwater Brewery
237 Joseph Campau, Detroit 48207
atwaterbeer.com
1175 Lakepointe St., Grosse Pointe Park 48230
inthepark1175.com

Detroit Beer Co.
1529 Broadway, Detroit 48226
detroitbeerco.com

Dragonmead Microbrewery
14600 E. 11 Mile Rd., Warren 48089
dragonmead.com

Jolly Pumpkin Artisan Ales
441 W. Canfield St., Detroit 48201
jollypumpkin.com

Kuhnhenn Brewing Co.
5919 Chicago Rd., Warren 48092
kbrewery.com

Liberty Street Brewing Co.
149 W. Liberty St., Plymouth 48170
libertystreetbeer.com

Motor City Brewing Works
470 W. Canfield St., Detroit 48201
motorcitybeer.com

Traffic Jam and Snug
511 W. Canfield St., Detroit 48201
trafficjamdetroit.com

INDULGE IN A DETROIT MAINSTAY:
CONEY DOGS

It surprises first-time visitors to learn that coney dogs are as important a food staple in Detroit as they are in New York. Brought to southeastern Michigan by Greek and Macedonian immigrants who passed first through Ellis Island and made contact with the Greek communities near Coney Island, coney dogs are ubiquitous in Detroit. And residents are as happy to argue about which dog is best as Kansas City's residents are to argue about the best BBQ. Dozens of coney restaurants lie scattered across the city, with both American Coney Island and Lafayette Coney Island claiming to have originated the dog in the Motor City. But virtually all dog stands follow a similar Detroit style: a natural casing wurst topped with a savory beef sauce, yellow mustard, and diced onions. Try a few and see which is your favorite.

American Coney Island
americanconeyisland.com

Lafayette Coney Island
118 W. Lafayette Blvd., Detroit 48226

Detroit One Coney Island
detroitoneconey.com

Leo's Coney Island
leosconeyisland.com

Joe's Top Dog
topdogconeyisland.com

National Coney Island
nationalconeyisland.com

SATISFY YOUR SWEET TOOTH
WITH SANDERS CHOCOLATES

Fred Sanders gave birth to Detroit's favorite candy in 1875. So popular were his chocolates, ice cream toppings, and pastries that Sanders Candy blossomed to include fifty-seven stores in the Great Lakes region at one time. Sanders's claim to fame was selling sweet treats such as candy, ice cream sundaes, and malted milk shakes—in fact, there's some evidence that Fred Sanders invented the nation's first ice cream soda when he substituted ice cream for the cream in his sodas—but light meals found their way to the menu too. Morley Candy Makers bought out Sanders in 2002, but Sanders Chocolates remains intact as do Fred's original recipes for mouthwatering chocolates. Take a tour at Morley's Clinton Township location to see how the candies are made, or pick up chocolates and ice cream toppings at one of eight Sanders locations throughout Detroit.

23770 Hall Rd., Clinton Township 48036
800-682-2760
sanderscandy.com

FIND STICK-TO-YOUR-RIBS COOKING
AT SOUL FOOD RESTAURANTS

Nearly 85 percent of the residents of the city of Detroit are of African American heritage, drawn to the Motor City around World War I when the automotive industry's labor shortage offered promises of economic and career advancement. And many of Detroit's African Americans came from the South, bringing with them the flavors of Memphis, Birmingham, New Orleans, and Jackson, Mississippi. As a result, Detroit's streets are blessed with a nice selection of good Southern and soul food restaurants serving barbecue and collards, fried chicken and okra, ribs and grits. Indulge in the meat-and-three offerings—and some more contemporary (even vegetarian or vegan) variations on this Southern menu—at soul food restaurants across the city serving slow-cooked meats, savory greens, rich macaroni and cheese, and sweet potato dishes.

Baker's Keyboard Lounge
20510 Livernois Ave., Detroit 48221
313-345-6300
theofficialbakerskeyboardlounge.com

Beans and Cornbread
29508 Northwestern Hwy., Southfield 48034
248-208-1680
beanscornbread.com

Cafe D'Mongo's Speakeasy
1439 Griswold St., Detroit 48226

Detroit Vegan Soul
8029 Agnes St., Detroit 48214
313-649-2759
detroitvegansoul.com

Steve's Soul Food
1440 Franklin St., Detroit 48207
313-393-0018
stevessoulfooddetroit.com

MAKE YOUR HAPPY HOUR HAPPIER
AT ONE OF DETROIT'S CRAFT DISTILLERIES

Prohibition lasted a good, long time in Detroit. The state of Michigan prohibited alcohol sales in 1916, a full three years before the federal government followed suit in 1919. But Detroiters are an industrious lot, accustomed to looking for an open window when a door closes. There's speculation that three-quarters of all the liquor that traveled into the US during the Prohibition era came through Detroit from Windsor, Canada, floating across the Detroit River in warm weather and driven across when the waterway froze. These days booze is not only legal in Detroit, it's downright trendy. Bars and restaurants across the city like mixing cocktails with locally distilled liquor. And Detroit's best distilleries each have their own tasting rooms, where you can sample the drinks neat or concocted into your favorite cocktail.

Valentine Distilling Co.
Small-batch vodkas, gins, bourbon whiskey, and
infused liquors
161 Vester Ave., Ferndale 48220
248-629-9951
valentinedistilling.com

Detroit City Distillery
Vodka, rye, whiskey, and gin distilled from locally
sourced ingredients
Eastern Market, 2462 Riopelle St., Detroit 48207
313-338-3760
detroitcitydistillery.com

Our/Detroit
Artisan vodka produced in a rehabbed billiard center
2545 Bagley Ave., Detroit 48216
313-656-4610
ourvodka.com/ourdetroit

Two James Spirits
Locally sourced whiskey, gin, vodka, and absinthe at
Detroit's first licensed distillery since Prohibition
2445 Michigan Ave., Detroit 48216
twojames.com

DISCOVER INDEPENDENT RESTAURANTS
IN BURGEONING MIDTOWN

When people talk about the revitalization of Detroit, it's Midtown they have in mind. Not too many years ago this section of Detroit, stretching roughly from Grand Circus Park near downtown to West Grand Boulevard in the north, was devoid of economic activity save the Cultural District, with its collection of top-notch museums, and Wayne State University. These days Midtown is smoking hot thanks to a partnership of public and private investors. The businesses popping up are steered largely by Detroiters who refused to give up on their city and they range from specialty boutiques selling artist- and designer-made clothing to microbreweries, locally crafted art galleries, and independently owned restaurants, as often as not with menus reliant on produce and herbs grown in Detroit's urban gardens.

Detroit Pizza Company
15 E. Kirby St., Suite 115, Detroit 48202
313-872-9000
thedetroitpizzaco.com

Go! Sy Thai
4240 Cass Ave., Suite 103, Detroit 48201
313-638-1467
gosythai.com

Maccabees at Midtown
5057 Woodward Ave., Detroit 48202
313-831-9311
facebook.com/MaccabeesAtMidtown

Selden Standard
3921 2nd Ave., Detroit 48201
313-438-5055
seldenstandard.com

Slows To Go
4107 Cass Ave., Detroit 48201
877-569-7246
slowstogo.com

Traffic Jam & Snug
511 W. Canfield St., Detroit 48201
313-831-9470
trafficjamdetroit.com

EAT SQUARE PIZZA
AT BUDDY'S

Pizza often comes square-shaped in Detroit, but Buddy's started it all in 1946. Actually, the restaurant traces its roots to 1936 when Buddy's launched as a neighborhood tavern and a blind pig, skirting federal alcohol laws by serving booze without a license. In the mid-1940s Buddy's went legit, selling their alcohol legally and, in an effort to further boost sales during a World War II downturn, they began baking Sicilian pies, which are traditionally square. The Sicilian-style pizza caught on. Other restaurants will dish up their own square zas, but you'll have to go to Buddy's to find the real deal, a pie that is consistently voted Detroit's best pizza. Other offerings include salads, sandwiches, and pasta. The restaurant's original location sits in Farmington Hills but these days Buddy's has locations across the city.

Farmington Hills and numerous metro Detroit locations
800-965-0505
buddyspizza.com

EAT DESSERT, DO GOOD
AT DETROIT WATER ICE FACTORY

A project launched by author and journalist Mitch Albom, Detroit Water Ice melds good food and good works in one tasty cup. Albom, who has spent some thirty years on the staff at the *Detroit Free Press* and has authored such books as *Tuesdays with Morrie* and *The Five People You Meet in Heaven,* grew up in Philadelphia and New Jersey, where this ancient Italian ice still thrives and where Mitch acquired his recipes. Water ice is something of a cross between sorbet and gelato, rich and thick and available in Motor City-themed flavors like Corvette Cherry, Motown Mint and the Chips, and Woodward Watermelon. If the dessert's yumminess isn't enough to tempt you, maybe this will: all profits from this store go to Detroit-based charitable projects, such as a medical clinic for homeless children and newly refurbished homes for Detroit-area poor working families.

1014 Woodward Ave., Detroit 48226
313-888-9106
detroitwaterice.com

INDULGE IN MIDDLE EASTERN FOOD
IN DEARBORN

Metro Detroit is home to more people of Arab descent than anyplace outside of the Middle East, with most of them calling Dearborn home. In fact, some 40 percent of Dearborn's residents hail from the Middle East, with most from Lebanon but others from Palestine, Pakistan, Jordan, Syria, and Iraq. Originally drawn by Detroit's automotive industry, these immigrants brought with them a collection of mouthwatering dishes that have made their way onto the city's restaurant menus. Expect recipes brought over from the Old Country, served by extraordinarily hospitable first- or second-generation Americans in family-owned restaurants, many of them located along Dearborn's main drag, Michigan Avenue. Dig into steaming-hot pita, fresh hummus, savory shawarma and kebabs, fresh fattoush, and kibbeh. This promises to be the best Middle Eastern cuisine you'll ever sink your teeth into.

Al Ameer
12710 W. Warren Ave., Dearborn 48126
313-582-8185
alameerrestaurant.com

Amani's Lebanese Restaurant
13823 Michigan Ave., Dearborn 48126
313-584-1890
amanilebaneserestaurant.com

Bucharest Grill
2040 Park Ave., Detroit 48226
1623 Michigan Ave., Detroit 48216 (takeout only)
313-965-3111
Bucharestgrill.com

Habib's
14316 Michigan Ave., Dearborn 48126
313-584-1515
habibscuisine.com

La Pita
22681 Newman St., Dearborn 48124
313-563-7482
lapitadearborn.com

M&M Cafe
13714 Michigan Ave., Dearborn 48126
313-581-577

RELIVE TIGERS HISTORY
AT THE CORNER TAP ROOM

If you're old enough to remember the old Tiger Stadium (once located in Corktown, replaced with downtown's Comerica Park in 2000), you'll enjoy dining at the Corner Tap Room. The restaurant honors the old stadium at Michigan and Trumbull with lots of retro Tigers displays. Many of the items on the walls and in the restaurant's glass display cases are replicas rather than authentic memorabilia. Still, the replica scoreboard and street sign, old uniforms, ball gloves, and programs conjure up fond memories for Tigers die-hards. As for the restaurant's menu, creative, hearty salads and ballpark-inspired dishes are the norm: loaded fries, a jalapeno beef and cheddar sandwich, and a bacon-wrapped dog. The Corner Tap Room sits near Comerica's Gate A and is open for lunch and dinner even when the stadium isn't.

Comerica Park
2100 Woodward Ave., Detroit 48201
313-962-4000
detroit.tigers.mlb.com/det/ballpark/

TIP
The Corner Tap Room is owned by Comerica's concessionaire. That means if you're going to a Tigers game you can buy a beer in the stadium and bring it into the restaurant. Alternately, you can buy a beer at the Corner Tap Room and bring it into the stands in time for the first pitch.

ENJOY THE VIEW WITH YOUR SWEETIE
AT COACH INSIGNIA ✗

Set at the tippy-top of the Renaissance Center, a collection of skyscrapers forming the centerpiece of Detroit's skyline and housing General Motors's headquarters, Coach Insignia is voted Detroit's Most Romantic Restaurant nearly every year and with good reason. The restaurant towers seven hundred feet above the Detroit River, taking in unforgettable views of the sparkling Detroit skyline, the Detroit River, and the city of Windsor, Ontario, to the south. Once upon a time, under different management, this restaurant rotated. That's no longer the case. But whatever is lost by being forced to gaze at the same sparkling view all evening long is gained in a top-notch menu and a mind-dizzying wine list. Premium steak and seafood is the norm as well as a handful of poultry and vegetarian dishes.

Renaissance Center, Floors 71 and 72, Detroit 48243
313-567-2622

TIP
The Detroit Marriott at the Renaissance Center is located within the same complex as Coach Insignia. If you're overnighting in Detroit, find out whether the hotel offers any specially priced hotel/dinner packages.

GET YOUR FETA FIX
AT GREEKTOWN

Located just east of Detroit's downtown, Greektown was, as its name suggests, the historic neighborhood of the city's Greek residents in the early 1900s. The city's new immigrants made their mark on the neighborhood with family-owned restaurants, bakeries, bars, and markets. As commercialization began to creep into the community, many Greeks moved on to more spacious digs in the suburbs. But the popular ethnic restaurants and shops they left behind remained largely intact and active. In the 1960s the neighborhood was redeveloped as a dining and entertainment district, which remains wildly popular today. These days it's casino-goers—the Greektown Casino is always a big draw—and Tigers fans who frequent the neighborhood's restaurants and bars, the latter coming to celebrate (or pout about) the result of the game in Comerica Park just blocks away.

Golden Fleece
525 Monroe Ave., Detroit 48226
313-962-7093

Pegasus Taverna
558 Monroe St., Detroit 48226
313-964-6800
pegasustavernas.com

Santorini Estiatorio
501 Monroe St., Detroit 48226
313-962-9366
santorinidetroit.com

BLOW YOUR DIET
AT GREEKTOWN'S ASTORIA PASTRY SHOP

Hands down the most beloved bakery in the city of Detroit, Astoria tempts visitors with colorful macaroons, flaky croissants, photo-worthy cupcakes, and decadent German chocolate tortes. More than one hundred pastries fill the menu at this confectionery in Detroit's Greektown, the historic neighborhood of the city's Greek residents since the turn of the twentieth century and now one of Detroit's most popular entertainment districts. Astoria opened its doors in 1971, launched by the Greek Teftis family. Ever since, the bakery has been awarded people's choice awards year after year by metro Detroiters. Astoria's Greek roots are still evident in its lengthy menu, which includes such specialties as baklava, choureki (a sweet egg bread), spinach pies, and a variety of Greek cookies. Eat in or take out.

541 Monroe, Detroit 48226
313-963-9603

320 S. Main, Royal Oak 48067
248-582-9220

astoriapastryshop.com

CELEBRATE RED WINGS HISTORY
AT HOCKEYTOWN CAFE

Hockeytown's three floors of dining space and a rooftop patio make this spot one of the largest in downtown Detroit. But even with all of that room, the Red Wings-themed restaurant overflows with fans on game day, all of them eager to pore over memorabilia while they wait for their burgers or pizzas to arrive. Display cases house the archival photos and jerseys of Red Wings teams of yore. And why not? The Wings's postseason playoff streak of twenty-four years stands as the longest active playoff streak of any of the four major American professional sports. But if hockey fans flock to this Woodward Avenue restaurant on game day, so do Tigers fans looking for pre- or postgame meals. Hockeytown's location right across the street from Comerica Park makes it a natural stop.

2301 Woodward Ave., Detroit 48201
313-965-9500
hockeytowncafe.com

TIP
Going to a Tigers game? Leave your car at the hotel, travel via the People Mover to the Grand Circus Park stop, and walk across to the game after lunch at Hockeytown.

FEED YOUR INNER CARNIVORE
AT ROAST

This fine dining restaurant in the Westin Book Cadillac Hotel, a restored 1920s-era hotel in downtown Detroit, has garnered one award after another since its opening in 2008. Roast is one of a host of restaurants under the direction of Cleveland-based chef Michael Symon, an Ohio restaurateur and Food Network Iron Chef star. As the name suggests, the dinner-only restaurant specializes in succulent, slow-roasted meats with its chief specialty being premium dry-aged steaks, filets, and pork chops. But you'll also find lamb, poultry, and a smattering of seafood and vegetarian dishes on the menu. Oenophiles: the wine list will keep you occupied for ages if you let it. Beer drinkers: Roast has won multiple awards for its interesting and lengthy taps list.

1128 Washington Blvd., Detroit 48226
313-961-2500
roastdetroit.com

TIP
If you're game for something different, ask about Roast's daily "roast beast," a rotating meat based on market availability. Offerings typically range from pork to wild boar and goat.

GET YOUR CAFFEINE BUZZ
AT ASTRO COFFEE

Rich, impeccably roasted pour-over coffee, organic pastries, and sandwiches and free Wi-Fi attract young creative types to this popular coffee shop in Corktown, once the home of Detroit's Irish population and now the site of some of the city's most interesting independently owned restaurants. But it's more than good coffee and baked goods that keep customers coming back. The vibe at Astro is so friendly and comfortable and the coffee is so good that patrons like to linger. Blackboard walls cover most of the cafe's interior, advertising the day's coffee and food menus as well as adding a splash of color with cheerful, vibrant chalk drawings of flower bouquets and the like. Astro was founded by two employees of London's revered Monmouth Coffee Company, but their love for the Motor City drew them to Corktown for good.

2124 Michigan Ave., Detroit 48216
313-808-0351
astrodetroit.com

FILL UP ON DINER STAPLES
AT ELWOOD BAR & GRILL

In 1936 the Elwood went up on Elizabeth Street and Woodward Avenue, the two street names combining to form the new restaurant's name, Elwood. Some sixty years later the city's most recognizable diner faced demolition, sitting as it was in the space designated for the Tigers's new home, Comerica Park. But the Elwood was so beloved that the building was instead moved to its current location, where the staff serves up platters of typical diner food: burgers, salads, grilled cheese sandwiches, hand-cut fries, and a Detroit mainstay, the coney dog, topped with chili and onions. Expect a bit of a wait if you visit on game day. The beloved art deco gem, with its familiar enameled steel facade and red neon sign, sits between Comerica and Ford Field and fills quickly with baseball and football fans.

300 E. Adams Ave., Detroit 48226
313-962-2337
elwoodgrill.com

TIP
The owners of the Elwood Bar & Grill love Detroit sports. Whatever their opening hours, you can expect the diner to be open for about an hour after Tigers and Lions home games.

QUENCH YOUR THIRST WITH A MICHIGAN-MADE BEER
AT GRAND TRUNK PUB

History runs deep in this downtown pub, from its origins as Traub Brothers Jewelry in 1879 to its transformation into a Grand Trunk Railway ticket office in 1910. There's even an unsubstantiated rumor that Harry Houdini operated a magic shop out of this location back in the day. The Grand Trunk has served as a restaurant and bar since the mid-1930s and there's plenty of the historic building's old architecture remaining, including vaulted ceilings, a heavy wooden bar, and century-old exposed brick walls. Michigan-sourced entrées like Two James meatloaf (named for the local whiskey in the gravy) and Ghetto Blaster beer battered fish and chips (another local drink) fill a menu that is rather more polished than your standard pub grub. More than 170 beers are on offer all the time, the vast majority of them brewed in Michigan.

612 Woodward Ave., Detroit 48226
313-961-3043
grandtrunkpub.com

TIP

Grand Trunk's central location within walking distance of Campus Martius, Hart Plaza, the Fox Theatre, and Comerica Park makes this a good stop for meals or a drink before or after a show or a baseball game.

PICK YOUR OWN STRAWBERRIES
(OR CHERRIES OR APPLES OR PUMPKINS) AT WESTVIEW ORCHARDS

There's one reason after another—or rather, one fruit after another —to keep visitors returning to this U-pick farm founded north of Detroit in 1813. The farm's harvest begins in early June with the strawberry crop. Once the strawberries begin to fade, Westview's cherries take their place followed soon after by peaches, apples, and, in late September, pumpkins. Not interested in picking your own fruit? Westview's Farm Market is open daily from May through December, selling farm-grown produce. Other treats at Westview render the orchard worthy of several hours of your time. Families enjoy visiting the restored 1869 schoolhouse, the goats and calves in the petting zoo, and farm tours via tractor-driven wagon. Adults sample house-made fruit wines. And the orchard's homemade baked goods, particularly their donuts, are popular with all ages.

65075 Van Dyke Rd., Washington 48095
586-752-3123
westvieworchards.com

MUSIC AND ENTERTAINMENT

CATCH
THE BEST LIVE MUSIC
AT THE MAJESTIC THEATRE

The Majestic doesn't look like much from the outside, although you can see glimpses of its former glory. Set within Detroit's up-and-coming Midtown neighborhood, the historic building ranked as the largest vaudeville theater in the world when it was constructed in 1915, and a pretty ornate one at that. But in spite of the Majestic's time-worn look, this one-thousand-seat theater is the place to be for live music in Detroit. The Majestic has built a reputation for hosting tomorrow's stars today, with a penchant for spotting performers that are on their way up. Previous acts have included the Black Keys, the Flaming Lips, George Clinton, Patti Smith, Sheryl Crow, Wilco, and many more. Located within the same building are restaurants and two other popular entertainment venues: the Garden Bowl (a historic bowling alley) and Populux (a smaller techno music venue).

4120 Woodward Ave., Detroit 48201
313-833-9700
majesticdetroit.com

ROCK-N-BOWL
WITH LIVE DJs
AT GARDEN BOWL

The nation's oldest active bowling center opened its doors in 1913 and the Garden Bowl has been drawing Detroiters ever since. The Garden Bowl's sixteen lanes, each of them outfitted with their original Brunswick pin-setting machines, glow in the dark, making them especially fun after hours. For a real kick, book a Rock-n-Bowl party with live DJing, pizza, soft drinks, and cocktails, disco balls, and, of course, glow bowling. The Garden Bowl sits in the heart of Midtown, a neighborhood that has been redeveloping rapidly during Detroit's recent revitalization efforts. Attached to the Garden Bowl building are a couple of casual burger-and-pizza restaurants, the Majestic Theatre (one of Detroit's most popular live music venues), and upstairs the newly refurbished Populux (a club that attracts an electronic- and techno-loving crowd).

4140 Woodward Ave., Detroit 48201
313-833-9700
majesticdetroit.com

DANCE TO TECHNO IN THE CITY THAT INVENTED IT
AT POPULUX

The little square of real estate occupied by Populux has a long history in Detroit's music annals. For years the home of the Magic Stick, a pool hall and small live music venue, this stage has hosted plenty of up-and-coming artists over the years including the White Stripes, Jack Johnson, and Kid Rock. But by early 2015 the storied venue had become decidedly dingy. An overhaul updated the space, brightening the room with multicolored LED lights and revamping its music mix to include electronic, techno, and house music. Populux is part of a larger entertainment complex on busy Woodward Avenue in Midtown. Also located within the building are a couple of casual restaurants, the larger live music venue the Majestic Theatre, and downstairs, the Garden Bowl, the nation's oldest active bowling center.

4140 Woodward Ave., Detroit 48201
313-833-9700
populuxdetroit.com

TAP YOUR TOES
AT THE MOTOWN MUSEUM

The musical icons of a generation all found early success at this humble house on Detroit's West Grand Boulevard, formerly the headquarters of Berry Gordy's Motown music label. Following the techniques of Detroit's automotive industry, Gordy brought hundreds of talented, unpolished young performers through the doors at Motown, taught them music, poise, and performance skills and sent them out into the world as some of the most accomplished singers in American history. Exhibits at the Motown Museum display album art, music and video clips, memorabilia, and costumes worn by Motown's biggest stars. Visitors also get the opportunity to walk through Motown's offices and to see the studio where its finest performers recorded their music: Smokey Robinson, Stevie Wonder, Diana Ross, Gladys Knight, Marvin Gaye, the Temptations, Michael Jackson, and many others.

2648 W. Grand Blvd., Detroit 48208
313-875-2264
motownmuseum.org

CATCH A CONCERT
AT CAMPUS MARTIUS PARK

Way back in 1788, Detroit's military recruits trained at the city's Campus Martius, which in Latin means "military ground." More than two centuries later, this two-and-a-half-acre public square in downtown Detroit serves as the city's gathering space. Surrounded by office towers and shopping centers, Campus Martius serves as a small green respite for work colleagues looking for a little break from their routine. Fountains, retractable stages, and a whole lot of green space attract families every season of the year. In the warm weather months, gather at Campus Martius for summertime festivals, live music, and theatrical performances. In winter, look for a public ice rink (and a warming tent), holiday carolers, Detroit's sixty-foot sparkling Christmas tree, winter festivals, and professional ice skating performances. Cafe tables and bistros provide a space to meet friends and colleagues year-round.

800 Woodward Ave., Detroit 48226
313-962-0101
campusmartiuspark.org

ENJOY THE WORLD'S LARGEST FREE JAZZ FESTIVAL
AT THE DETROIT JAZZ FESTIVAL

Each Labor Day weekend, Hart Plaza and Campus Martius in downtown Detroit come alive with the sounds of world-class jazz. The festival was launched in 1980, part of an effort to bring world-class music to Detroit and to encourage people to visit downtown. In its early years, the Detroit Jazz Festival partnered with the highly acclaimed international jazz festival in Montreux, Switzerland, sharing performers and even collaborating on poster art. These days the Detroit Jazz Festival stands alone, featuring more than one hundred artists performing in concert on five stages spread along Woodward from Hart Plaza on the Detroit River up to Campus Martius several blocks to the north. Besides live music performances, the festival includes food tents, music education for kids and adults, unique jam sessions, and opportunities to meet and greet some of jazz's most accomplished artists.

detroitjazzfest.com

TEMPT LADY LUCK
AT DETROIT'S CASINOS

Detroit's three downtown casinos all share the characteristics of Las Vegas gaming centers—resort hotels, multiple fine and casual dining options, plenty of premium games, and theaters that draw a wide variety of entertainers. But each casino offers its own style. MGM Grand opened its doors as Detroit's first Las Vegas-style casino, an art deco resort with exceptional service. Greektown's thirty-story luminescent blue tower adds a striking focal point to that downtown entertainment district. MotorCity is the only locally owned casino. Created by noted automotive designer Chip Foose in a Future Retro style, MotorCity's neon and sleek lines pay homage to Detroit and America's enchantment with the automobile. Each of the casinos' premium restaurants and hotels ranks among some of the best in The D.

Greektown Casino

The blue tower and glittering gold lobby of the Greektown Casino stand out in Detroit's Greektown neighborhood, one of the city's most popular entertainment districts. The casino hotel's proximity to the Greektown People Mover stop makes it easy to travel car-free to other Detroit downtown attractions.

555 E. Lafayette Ave., Detroit 48226
877-424-5554
greektowncasino.com

MGM Grand Detroit

MGM Grand's premium restaurant, Wolfgang Puck Steak, garners a lot of attention, but just as popular is TAP, a Detroit sports-themed pub with loads of autographed memorabilia. When you aren't at the slots or gaming tables, check out MGM's luxury spa, Immerse.

1777 Third St., Detroit 48226
877-888-2121
mgmgranddetroit.com

MotorCity Casino

Dinner at MotorCity's Iridescence restaurant is impressive, paired with an award-winning wine list and sweeping views of the Detroit skyline and the Ambassador Bridge to Windsor. Detroit-themed treatments fill the D.Tour spa menu, including the Pink Cadillac Body Wrap.

2901 Grand River Ave., Detroit 48201
866-782-9622
motorcitycasino.com

SEE THE SOARING, OVERSIZED BALLOONS
AT AMERICA'S THANKSGIVING PARADE

Each Thanksgiving morning, Detroiters head downtown for America's Thanksgiving Parade, a beloved part of Detroit's holiday season since 1924. Giant helium-filled balloons, colorful floats, scores of marching bands, and a colorful Distinguished Clown Corps of more than two thousand move through the city streets to welcome the start of another holiday season. If you're feeling energetic, join in Detroit's Turkey Trot 5K and 10K, the nation's largest Thanksgiving morning race, which begins just hours before the parade kicks off. In the off-season, the Parade Company's warehouse tours in Hamtramck are popular. Visitors learn about the complicated logistics behind the parade, see the world's largest collection of papier-mâché heads, check out the imaginative floats and more than three thousand costumes in storage, and get a look at the costume shop that creates all of the performers' regalia.

theparade.org

TAKE IN
A CONCERT, MUSICAL,
OR BROADWAY SHOW
AT THE ORNATE FOX AND FISHER THEATRES

The two crown jewels in Detroit's entertainment scene, the Fox Theatre and the Fisher Theatre, were both opened to the public in 1928. The Fox, located in the heart of downtown as part of the Fox Theatre chain, was an over-the-top movie palace built with vibrant Persian, Chinese, and Indian motifs; a thirteen-foot-diameter crystal chandelier; and gold embellishments from around the globe. A thorough renovation in 1988 restored the theater's original grandeur and opened the venue for headliner concerts, musicals, and ballets. A bit farther north, the ornate Fisher Theatre sits within the Fisher Building, an art deco masterpiece designed by Albert Kahn largely for office and retail space. In the theater's early years it was known for its collection of macaws that would stroll through the audience looking for handheld treats. These days it's Broadway-style shows that fill the seats at the Fisher Theatre, which is about half the size of the Fox and designed in an exuberant Mayan Revival style.

Fox Theatre
2211 Woodward Ave., Detroit 48201
313-471-3200
olympiaentertainment.com

Fisher Theatre
3011 W. Grand Blvd., Detroit 48202
313-872-1000
broadwayindetroit.com

REVEL IN RAVEL
AT THE DETROIT OPERA HOUSE

The Capitol Theatre claimed to be the fifth-largest theater in the world when it was unveiled to all of Detroit in 1922. Decorated in the Italian Renaissance style, furnished with state-of-the-art acoustics, and patterned after the grand opera houses of Europe, it's no surprise that in the late 1990s, when the Detroit Opera House was renovated, the Michigan Opera Theatre claimed the space as its home. Time-tested operatic works are commonly performed at the downtown Detroit Opera House as are more contemporary musical shows. But the theater also offers a wide selection of headliner musical concerts as well as an array of dance performances, ranging from classical ballets like *The Nutcracker* and *Swan Lake* to *Dracula, Where the Wild Things Are,* and contemporary African American dance.

1526 Broadway, Detroit 48226
313-961-3500
michiganopera.org

GROOVE TO WORLD-CLASS JAZZ
AT CLIFF BELL'S

Cliff Bell got his start in the hospitality business at the tender age of sixteen, first working at his father's pub and later, during the Prohibition years, opening and managing a string of Detroit speakeasies. But eventually the entrepreneur's claim to fame would be the club that bore his name, Cliff Bell's. Noteworthy in the 1930s for its state-of-the-art air conditioning, Cliff Bell's is famous today as one of the oldest and most highly respected jazz clubs in the nation. Enjoy drinks and appetizers or order a full dinner menu that includes a decent selection of vegetarian options. The golden glow of polished mahogany and brass makes visitors feel warm and cozy as soon as they step inside. The live jazz acts on stage each evening—many of them native Detroiters who've made it big—keep the crowds coming back.

2030 Park Ave., Detroit 48226
313-961-2543
cliffbells.com

TIP
Cliff Bell's is famous for its music. Expect a crowd (make a reservation) and expect to pay a cover even if you arrive before the band starts.

CATCH A CONCERT
AT THE MEADOW BROOK
MUSIC FESTIVAL

Each summer music fans gather to hear live music under the stars at Meadow Brook, an outdoor amphitheater on the campus of Oakland University in Detroit's northern suburbs. This scenic piece of property originally belonged to automotive innovator and manufacturer John F. Dodge. In 1964, Dodge's family gifted the land to the university as the summertime outdoor venue for Detroit Symphony Orchestra concerts. In 1968 the performance schedule expanded to include ballet and by the early '70s rock 'n' roll made its way onto the Meadow Brook calendar. The DSO still performs at Meadow Brook regularly, but you can expect a wide variety of performers all season long, from May to September, from Tony Bennett and Diana Krall to Lady Gaga and Flogging Molly.

Oakland University, 3554 Walton Blvd., Rochester Hills 48309
248-377-0100
palacenet.com

HEAR ONE OF THE WORLD'S MOST LISTENED-TO ORCHESTRAS,
THE DETROIT SYMPHONY ORCHESTRA

The DSO began entertaining Detroit way back in 1887, making this the fourth-oldest orchestra in the US. Such notable artists as Igor Stravinsky, Richard Strauss, Sergei Rachmaninoff, and Isadora Duncan helped cement the DSO's reputation for quality. Those headliners and the orchestra's apparently perennial interest in making its music more accessible to the public have made the DSO one of the world's most famous. In 1922 the orchestra became the first ever to broadcast over the radio. In the 1930s the DSO was the official orchestra for the *Ford Sunday Evening Hour* radio show, and in the 1960s many orchestra members played backup on Motown chart-toppers. In 2011 the DSO launched the world's first free orchestra webcast, *Live from Orchestra Hall.* Classical and pop music concerts—even a concert series for children as young as age two—are performed at the Max M. and Marjorie S. Fisher Music Center.

3711 Woodward Ave., Detroit 48201
313-576-5111
dso.org

GROOVE
AT THE WORLD'S OLDEST JAZZ CLUB, BAKER'S KEYBOARD LOUNGE

Opened in 1933 by Chris and Fannie Baker as a sandwich restaurant, Baker's developed a reputation for its entertainment in record-breaking time owing to the passion of the Bakers's son. Clarence, who had a thing for jazz piano, just couldn't seem to resist booking live music and before long it was Baker's keyboards rather than its sandwiches that were drawing crowds. The small art deco club northwest of downtown has a full dinner menu, an attractive keyboard-inspired bar, and intimate seating for just ninety-nine. But the best reason to visit Baker's is its musical pedigree, a history that reads like an honest-to-goodness who's who of jazz: John Coltrane, Louis Armstrong, Cab Calloway, Dave Brubeck, Miles Davis, Ella Fitzgerald, and many, many others. Expect live jazz every night of the week except Monday, when Baker's is closed.

20510 Livernois Ave., Detroit 48221
313-345-6300
theofficialbakerskeyboardlounge.com

JOIN FIFTEEN THOUSAND OF YOUR CLOSEST FRIENDS JAMMING
AT THE DTE ENERGY MUSIC THEATRE

Michigan's premier outdoor concert venue hosts scores of rock and country icons each summer. With a capacity of more than fifteen thousand (including pavilion and lawn seats), the outdoor amphitheater originally known as Pine Knob opened in 1972 and ranks among the largest amphitheaters in the nation. Since 1992 DTE Energy Music Theatre has kicked off its season Memorial Day weekend with classic rock singer Eddie Money. He continues to make his appearance each year followed by a season that includes approximately fifty acts such as Lady Antebellum, the Dave Matthews Band, Neil Young, Nicki Minaj, and Kid Rock, a hometown boy and perennial favorite among Detroit concertgoers. DTE Energy Music Theatre's season runs from May to late September or October.

7774 Sashabaw Rd., Clarkston 48348
248-377-0100
palacenet.com

WATCH A PLAY
AT THE GEM AND CENTURY THEATRES

The Century Theatre traces its roots to 1902 when a group of socially prominent Detroit ladies constructed a new gathering space, the mission-style Twentieth Century Club. About twenty years later, the socialites decided they needed a theater and hired George Mason to build a Spanish Revival addition to their club. Taken together, this duplex of early twentieth-century buildings today comprises the Gem and Century Theatres, the former with traditional row and aisle seating and the latter with cabaret-style seating. In 1997 the attractive brick and sandstone building made its way into the Guinness Book of World Records when the five-million-pound structure became the heaviest building ever moved on wheels. The relocation was made necessary by the decision to build the Detroit Tigers's new stadium, Comerica Park, downtown. The two theaters each seat about two hundred people and share a common lobby. There's also a restaurant on-site.

333 Madison Ave., Detroit 48226
313-963-9800
gemtheatre.com

FEEL THE ENERGY
AT MOVEMENT ELECTRONIC MUSIC FESTIVAL

For one glorious weekend in May all of downtown Detroit pulses with the music of Movement, an internationally recognized electronic music extravaganza. More than one hundred artists—local celebs as well as innovators in the field of electronic music—perform on five stages in downtown's Hart Plaza, set right on the banks of the Detroit River. Also part of the event is a physical art project that encourages artists to submit pieces for display at the festival before disseminating them in communities across the metro area. Launched as the Detroit Electronic Music Festival back in 2000—and still referred to as DEMF by many—the festival takes place from Friday through Monday each Memorial Day weekend in the city that invented techno music. A one-day or full weekend wristband makes it possible to come and go to a variety of music events.

Hart Plaza, Detroit 48226
248-584-1646
movement.us

ADMIRE THE WORLD'S HOTTEST MUSCLE CARS
AT THE WOODWARD DREAM CRUISE

What started as a fundraising idea to earn money for a community children's soccer field has morphed into the largest one-day automotive event in the world. The Woodward Dream Cruise attracts 1.5 million visitors from across the globe each year to a sixteen-mile parade of more than fifty thousand restored cars, all of them built in Detroit's automotive heydays of the 1950s and '60s. Smokin' hot Corvettes, Mustangs, and other muscle cars share the road with beautifully restored Edsels, Studebakers, and Corvairs on a cruise down America's first highway, Highway 1, an extension of Detroit's Woodward Avenue. The Dream Cruise lasts about twelve hours and takes place every year on the third Saturday in August.

Woodward Ave. between Ferndale and Pontiac
248-672-6118
woodwarddreamcruise.com

CATCH A HEADLINER
AT THE PALACE OF AUBURN HILLS

The Palace ranks as Detroit's premier professional sports and concert venue. Since its construction in 1988 in Detroit's northern suburbs, the Palace has been home court to the NBA's Detroit Pistons. When the fans aren't shouting, "Dee-Troit Basketball!" the arena is used to host world-class performances of marquee artists like Rihanna, the Doobie Brothers, Michael Flatley, and Iron Maiden. More unusual events that take place at the Palace include Cirque du Soleil shows, indoor rodeos, wrestling, and even sno-cross events, where stunt-performing snowmobiles race and leap over mountains of artificially made snow. The Palace is a sister property with the outdoor venues DTE Energy Music Theatre and Meadow Brook Amphitheatre.

2 Isiah Thomas Dr., Auburn Hills 48322
248-377-8221
palacenet.com

SPORTS AND RECREATION

WATCH FOR FLYING OCTOPI
AT THE JOE LOUIS ARENA

It's a Detroit tradition that began in 1952, when eight play-off wins earned a hockey team the NHL Stanley Cup. Two brothers tossed an octopus onto the ice at a Red Wings game, the creature's eight legs symbolizing the necessary wins, and voila! The Wings swept the series. The octopus has been seen as a good luck charm in Detroit ever since. Through the 2016-17 season you can catch the Wings at Joe Louis Arena, named for the heavyweight boxing champ who lived most of his life in the Motor City. In 2017 the Red Wings will move to a brand-new downtown stadium in the heart of a newly developed fifty-block Arena District. Octopi are sure to be seen as lucky charms at the new arena too, but don't think about bringing your own cephalopod to a game. You'll earn yourself a hefty fine if they catch you.

19 Steve Yzerman Dr., Detroit 48226
313-471-6606
olympiaentertainment.com

CHILL WITH THE PENGUINS
AT THE DETROIT ZOO

The world's largest penguinarium, the Detroit Zoo's new Polk Penguin Conservation Center, took center stage at its opening in the spring of 2016. Eighty penguins swim, dive, and waddle in a twenty-five-foot-deep diving tank and past underwater pedestrian tunnels, all housed in a building meant to resemble an iceberg. Penguins aren't the only cold weather animals with fantastic digs at the 125-acre Detroit Zoo. Other exhibits getting lots of attention are the Cotton Family Wolf Wilderness Exhibit, which in 2015 debuted the zoo's first wolves since the 1980s, and the Arctic Ring of Life, ranking as one of North America's largest polar bear habitats with its own dive tanks and underwater tunnels. In total the Detroit Zoo houses approximately twenty-five hundred additional animals, from lions, tigers, and bears to a year-round Butterfly Garden.

8450 W. 10 Mile Rd., Royal Oak 48067
248-541-5717
detroitzoo.org

RIDE THE CAROUSEL OR FERRIS WHEEL
AT COMERICA PARK

Admittedly, most people don't go to Comerica Park, home of the Detroit Tigers, solely for the amusement park rides. But since gates open ninety minutes before the first pitch, why not? Comerica's Tiger Carousel is furnished strictly with tigers (surprise, surprise!) and the little cars on the Fly Ball Ferris Wheel resemble baseballs. Both are open to kids and adults. If you've still got time to spare before the opening pitch, check out the Walk of Fame. The historical exhibit spreads across the park's main concourse, detailing Tiger baseball history all the way back to the 1880s. Six larger-than-life statues on the left field wall honor Detroit's standout players: Willie Horton, Ty Cobb, Charlie Gehringer, Hank Greenberg, Hal Newhouser, and Al Kaline.

2100 Woodward Ave., Detroit 48201
313-962-4000
detroit.tigers.mlb.com

RUN TO CANADA (AND BACK AGAIN)
AT THE DETROIT MARATHON

There aren't many marathon courses that promise the opportunity to run across international borders. The Detroit Free Press/Talmer Bank Marathon is one of them. Runners line up at the starting gate near COBO Center, then run into Canada via the Ambassador Bridge at around Mile 3. After a four-mile stretch in Windsor, Ontario, the route veers back into Michigan again, this time via the Detroit-Windsor Tunnel, which travels beneath the Detroit River. Other highlights along the 26.2-mile marathon route include the Detroit Riverwalk and Windsor Riverwalk, a circle around Belle Isle, the towers of GM's Renaissance Center, and at least a dozen live music stages to help pass the time. The Detroit Marathon is held annually in mid-October and includes the option of shorter distances: a US-only or international half marathon, a 5K, or a relay race. Don't forget your passport!

freepmarathon.com

PADDLE AROUND
THE DETROIT RIVER'S BELLE ISLE

Belle Isle has long been a green oasis for Detroiters, a quiet respite with a small zoo, a Great Lakes museum, fountains, an aquarium, picnic areas, and a swimming beach. In 2014 the state of Michigan acquired Belle Isle as its 102nd state park, a move that was met with some controversy. Whatever the politics of the decision, transitioning Belle Isle to state control has allowed for some major park infrastructure improvements including two canoe and kayak rentals, one at Belle Isle Beach and another at Lake Muskoday. Paddle around the island for picture-postcard views of Detroit's sparkling skyline, the towers of GM's Renaissance Center standing front and center, as well as photo ops of the Windsor riverfront and Milliken State Park's wetlands and lighthouse.

2 Inselruhe Ave., Detroit 48207
844-235-5375
belleisle.org

TIP
Now that Belle Isle is a Michigan state park, there is an entrance fee required to access the island.

CYCLE THE MOTOR CITY'S URBAN GARDENS
WITH WHEELHOUSE DETROIT

Detroit's urban gardens have gotten a lot of attention in recent years. A city whose population and subsequent need for single-family houses has declined precipitously in the past few decades, Detroit removed many of its abandoned houses and replaced the empty lots with topsoil and garden plots. Wheelhouse Detroit guides visitors to some of the city's most interesting green spaces, many of which provide the produce for the city's up-and-coming restaurants. Not into group tours? Rent a bike and pedal solo along the level Riverwalk or the paved rail-trail, the Dequindre Cut. It's hard to imagine a location better suited to bicycling, with views of the Detroit and Windsor skylines, the wetlands of Milliken State Park, and the lumbering freighters passing through the Detroit River.

Rivard Plaza on the Detroit Riverwalk, 1340 E. Atwater St., Detroit 48207
313-656-2453
wheelhousedetroit.com

CAMP, FISH, AND HUNT DOWNTOWN
AT THE OUTDOOR ADVENTURE CENTER

It can be hard to experience Michigan's great outdoors when you live in the heart of a major urban center. Where can you try your hand at camping? And how do you learn the necessary skills to fish? Enter the Outdoor Adventure Center. Located within the old Globe Building, a marine steam engine factory where the young Henry Ford once learned factory work, the Michigan Department of Natural Resources's OAC replicates the very best of Michigan's many outdoor experiences: hiking state park trails, viewing northern Michigan's towering waterfalls, or operating a fishing boat or a snowmobile. The aim is to give urban dwellers a taste of Michigan's recreational opportunities. Visit the OAC for a fun indoor family day trip or use the facility's resources and staff as a catalyst for planning your own outdoor adventure.

1801 Atwater St., Detroit 48207
844-622-6367
michigan.gov/oac

ENJOY A MORNING RUN
ALONG THE DETROIT
INTERNATIONAL RIVERWALK

Spanning three and a half miles from the Joe Louis Arena toward Belle Isle, the Detroit International Riverwalk ties together a host of riverfront gems: William G. Milliken State Park, Rivard Plaza, and the popular gathering place at Hart Plaza. This lovely green space is like a breath of fresh air in downtown Detroit, where just a few years ago the Detroit River lapped against an embarrassing array of abandoned parking lots and crumbling breakwaters. Today's Riverwalk includes outdoor amphitheaters, natural wetlands, a towering white lighthouse, a carousel, fountains, public art, colorful flower beds, marinas, and views of Windsor, Ontario, just across the water. The Riverwalk ranks as a favorite location for a morning run or a lunchtime stroll. Construction on the Riverwalk continues, heading west from the Joe Louis Arena to the Ambassador Bridge to Canada.

Rosa Parks Blvd. to the Belle Isle Bridge, Detroit 48226
313-566-8200
detroitriverfront.org

TIP
Would you rather bicycle the Riverwalk than navigate it on foot? Wheelhouse Detroit rents bikes at the Rivard Plaza near Atwater and Rivard Streets.

BICYCLE TO EASTERN MARKET
VIA THE DEQUINDRE CUT GREENWAY

Once an abandoned leg of the Grand Trunk Railroad Line, the Dequindre Cut extends northward the quiet, green space that has made Detroit's riverfront so pleasant in recent years. The one-and-a-half-mile paved urban recreation trail lies largely below street level and leads from the Detroit Riverwalk and the Outdoor Adventure Center in the south to the shops and neighborhoods around the historic Eastern Market. The path is divided into pedestrian and bicycle lanes and adorned with colorful art displays and graffiti, and while the route makes a great recreation area for many, some Detroiters have taken to using the "Cut" and the adjoining Riverwalk as a bicycle commuting route. The existing Dequindre Cut is just the beginning of a larger plan to one day expand the trail to a distance of twenty-seven miles.

Detroit Riverwalk to Gratiot Ave.
313-566-8200
detroitriverfront.org

CATCH A LIONS GAME
AT FORD FIELD

Okay, so the Lions haven't exactly been a fantastic NFL team in the past, oh . . . sixty years. They're one of only a handful of teams never to have played in the Super Bowl. But Detroiters are nothing if not loyal sports fans and win or lose, they love the Lions. The 65,000-seat covered stadium (which also hosts headliner concerts and one-off hockey events) was completed in 2002, two years after the Detroit Tigers unveiled their new downtown stadium just a few blocks away. When the Red Wings's new arena opens in 2017, three of Detroit's major league sports—football, baseball, and hockey—will all be located within an easy walk of Detroit's downtown hotels. (The Pistons play at the Palace in Auburn Hills.)

2000 Brush St., Detroit 48226
313-262-2000
detroitlions.com/ford-field

SEE WHERE BASEBALL'S GREATS MADE HISTORY
AT TIGER STADIUM FIELD

There's a fallow field in the heart of Detroit's Corktown. But it's no ordinary field. This green space at the corner of Michigan Avenue and Trumbull Street was the home of the Detroit Tigers from 1912 to 1999 (and the Detroit Lions from 1938 to1974). First occupied by Navin Field and Briggs Stadium, the site is best known as the location of Tiger Stadium. Despite a great deal of effort to save the old stadium, it was razed in 2008-09. But the ground still feels hallowed to a lot of Detroiters. So the ball diamond remains, the home field for several high school and college teams whose members play on the very field where greats like Hank Greenberg, Al Kaline, Ty Cobb, Willie Horton, and Mickey Lolich played and where Mark Fidrych talked to the baseball from the pitcher's mound. The park is closed to the public, but you can easily view the diamond through the chain-link fence and shoot photos of one of Detroit's sporting meccas.

Michigan Avenue at Trumbull Street

BICYCLE THE PERIMETER
OF BELLE ISLE STATE PARK

Surrounded by the Detroit River and located just four miles from downtown, Belle Isle's one thousand acres offer a quiet natural retreat for urban dwellers. Designated a Michigan state park in 2014 (you'll need to pay an entrance fee now) and accessible via the Douglas MacArthur Bridge, Belle Isle's list of pastimes ranges from picnicking within view of the attractive Detroit skyline to the Memorial Day Grand Prix IndyCar races around the park's paved streets. But one of the most popular ways to circumnavigate Belle Isle is on two wheels. The easy paved route passes a small zoo and aquarium, a swimming beach, a driving range, fountains, a Great Lakes museum, Lake Muskoday, and the Livingstone Memorial Lighthouse built in 1929. It is the only lighthouse in the nation constructed of marble.

2 Inselruhe Ave., Detroit 48207
844-235-5375
belleisle.org

TIP
Don't have your own bicycle with you? Rent a bike at Flynn Pavilion on Belle Isle or at Wheelhouse Detroit on the Detroit Riverwalk near Rivard Street.

LACE UP YOUR SKATES
AT THE CAMPUS MARTIUS ICE RINK

When the snow flies, downtown's Campus Martius Park transforms its lush, green north lawn into a wintertime recreation center. Surrounded by gleaming office towers, trees covered in a thousand glistening white lights, and, at holiday season, backed by the city's multicolored Christmas tree and its twenty-six-foot-high menorah, Campus Martius's ice rink is among the city's most popular downtown outdoor recreation facilities. The rink has hosted performances by numerous national and Olympic ice skating champions. But locals also enjoy strapping on their own skates (you can rent them on-site) and having a go around the rink themselves. The park's warming tent and its popular cafe, the Fountain Bistro, offer options for warming up when Detroit's wintertime weather proves too much.

800 Woodward Ave., Detroit 48226
313-962-0101
campusmartiuspark.org

TRY FEATHERBOWLING
AT THE CADIEUX CAFE

A remnant of a once popular Belgian sport, featherbowling lives at Detroit's Cadieux Cafe . . . and scarcely anywhere else in the world. To play the game, participants roll small wooden balls the length of a sixty-foot hard-packed dirt court in a competition resembling a cross between Bocci and Closest to the Pin. But there's no pin in this cafe, just a small pigeon feather jutting up from the earthen floor. Once a social hub for Detroiters of Belgian descent, Cadieux Cafe began its life as a Prohibition-era speakeasy. The restaurant's authentic Belgian roots are reflected not only in its featherbowling lanes but in its dinner menu too. Fill up on white-wine-steamed mussels, Belgian sausage, spinach mashed potatoes, and Belgian stew washed down, naturally, with a yeasty Belgian beer.

4300 Cadieux Rd., Detroit 48224
313-882-8560
cadieuxcafe.com

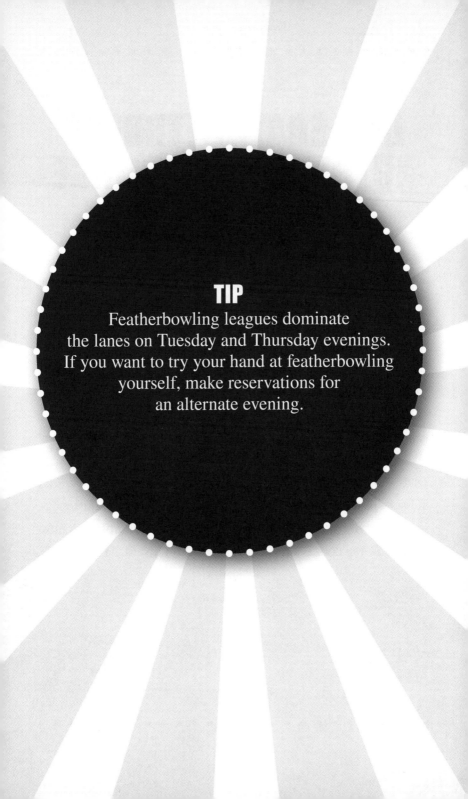

TIP

Featherbowling leagues dominate
the lanes on Tuesday and Thursday evenings.
If you want to try your hand at featherbowling
yourself, make reservations for
an alternate evening.

CELEBRATE DETROIT'S AUTOMOTIVE HERITAGE
AT AUTOPALOOZA

Beginning Memorial Day weekend, the greater Detroit area celebrates its century-long love affair with the automobile at Autopalooza. A wide array of events fill the summer-long party kicked off in May with the Grand Prix IndyCar race around Detroit's Belle Isle and followed shortly thereafter by NASCAR races at the Michigan International Speedway. A luxury vintage automobile show and auction, the Concours d'Elegance, takes place each year in Plymouth, drawing those who simply want to look at rare antique vehicles as well as those interested in buying. The Old Car Festival at Dearborn's Greenfield Village features models built between 1890 and 1932 on grounds that were once owned by Henry Ford himself. And there are multiple vintage car cruises from Eastpointe (near Lake St. Clair) to Westland in the western suburbs. The most popular Autopalooza cruise is the famous Woodward Dream Cruise.

Memorial Day through mid-September
autopalooza.org

GO SHREDDIN'
AT ALPINE VALLEY

Detroit isn't exactly mountainous, but Alpine Valley keeps area snowboarders happy nonetheless. Blessed with good, North Country snow in the depths of winter—plus some snowmaking equipment to augment when Mother Nature grows stingy—Alpine Valley draws schussers and boarders from across southeastern Michigan to the region's largest ski area. Four terrain parks, including a half pipe, are carved out of Alpine Valley's twelve-hundred-foot mountain, while skiers can take advantage of twenty-five tree-lined downhill ski slopes, eleven of them designed for beginners, eight for advanced skiers, and all of them serviced by nine chair lifts and four tow ropes. Alpine Valley provides rentals and lessons for every age group as well as a number of racing programs. The resort's Hornet's Nest lounge offers snacks, drinks, and occasional live music.

6775 Highland Rd., White Lake 48383
248-887-2180
skialpinevalley.com

TRY AN ORIGINAL DETROIT SPORT
AT THE FOWLING WAREHOUSE

It's one part bowling, one part Closest to the Pin, and one part football. It's fowling (rhymes with bowling), a sport invented by a local Detroiter. Located in a spacious warehouse in the village of Hamtramck, each lane is outfitted with ten pins laid out in standard triangles on both ends. Players face one another on opposite ends of the lanes and work at knocking down their opponent's pins by either throwing or bouncing the football down the lane. The winner is the one who knocks down all the pins first. The Fowling Warehouse has a stocked bar . . . which may or may not affect your game. But there's no food service on-site. Bring your own snacks or order pizza in.

3901 Christopher St., Hamtramck 48211
313-264-1288
fowlingwarehouse.com

TEE OFF ON HOLY GROUND
AT SHEPHERD'S HOLLOW GOLF CLUB

This lush 350-acre golf course in northwest Detroit was built on land formerly operated as the Colombiere Center, a retreat once used by the Detroit Province of the Society of Jesus, a Catholic order of priests. With its gently rolling hills, sparkling lakes, and beautiful hardwood trees, Shepherd's Hollow comes about as close to golfing heaven as you're likely to find in metro Detroit. Directional bunkers characterize the long, narrow, tree- and lake-bordered fairways. Par is seventy-two over 7,236 yards for the course's first eighteen holes and if that's not enough, play another nine. Shepherd's Hollow offers twenty-seven. After your game, linger over dinner at Shepherd's Hollow's white, colonnaded restaurant. Dine inside by the fireplace or out on the terrace on a meal created with produce grown in the resort's gardens.

9085 Big Lake Rd., Clarkston 48346
248-922-0300
shepherdshollow.com

LOOK UP AT THE FISH
AT SEA LIFE MICHIGAN AQUARIUM

Offering thirty exhibits and some five thousand animals on display, Sea Life Michigan joined a long list of kid-friendly metro Detroit attractions when it opened in 2015. Smiling sharks inhabit Shark Shipwreck. Glowing jellyfish, sea horses, and languorous octopi rank as favorite oddities. And a clear, underwater passageway gives Sea Life visitors the sense that they're strolling along the ocean floor looking up at hundreds of multicolored fish and sea turtles. Michigan's Great Lakes creatures find a home at Sea Life too, including trout, walleye, and perch. There's a strong emphasis on children at this aquarium, with informational iPad displays installed at kid height and Plexiglas observatories where little ones can poke their heads into tanks of colorful fish. Don't miss the staffed touch pool where visitors are permitted to pet crabs and starfish.

Great Lakes Crossing, 4316 Baldwin Rd., Auburn Hills 48326
866-622-0605
visitsealife.com/michigan

TIP
Headed to Sea Life with the kids? Make a day of it and spend time at Michigan's new LEGOLAND, new to Great Lakes Crossing in early 2016.

EXPERIENCE DETROIT'S WATERING HOLES
VIA MOTOR CITY BREW TOURS

One part education, one part outdoor recreation, and one part social hour, Motor City Brew Tours take suds-loving visitors on a journey through Detroit history, stopping for an adult beverage break here and there. Choose your activity level: you can take it easy and tour via bus or work up a little sweat traveling on foot or via bicycle. Tours follow themes such as Prohibition, Auto History or Highlights of Corktown and range from excursions within Detroit proper to tours of Royal Oak, Grosse Pointe, or Belle Isle. Whatever your destination or transportation of choice, the tours include stops and beer samples at three locally owned breweries, a full lunch, and ample supplies of snacks and water along the way. Tours take place year-round (except the bike tours—they run May to September).

248-850-2563
motorcitybrewtours.com

CULTURE AND HISTORY

GET TO KNOW DIEGO RIVERA
AT THE DETROIT INSTITUTE OF ARTS

The DIA became the source of numerous news stories just a few years ago, when Detroit's looming bankruptcy led to questions of whether the museum might be forced to sell some of its masterpieces to settle the city's debts. Thankfully, a grand bargain assured that the DIA's artworks would stay right where they are. Considered among the top six art collections in the US, the DIA's masterpieces include *Self Portrait,* the first Van Gogh to enter an American museum collection; Bruegel's *The Wedding Dance;* and sculpture by Italian artist Bernini. But the pièce de résistance is Diego Rivera's *Detroit Industry* murals covering all four walls of the Rivera Court. Painted in the 1930s, the murals are widely accepted as the finest Mexican murals in America and the work that Rivera himself considered his most successful. They also rank as the most popular artworks at the DIA.

5200 Woodward Ave., Detroit 48202
313-833-7900
dia.org

TIP

The DIA also has a reputation for offering some pretty great public events. . . most of them free. Visit Friday Night Live! for live music performances ranging from cabaret to classical. Other events include storytelling, hands-on art workshops, puppet theater, and artist demos.

DIG THROUGH AMERICAN HISTORY
AT THE HENRY FORD MUSEUM

Think of it as America's attic, spread across twelve acres. The Henry Ford Museum, begun as Ford's personal collection, contains a breathtaking array of Americana including George Washington's army cot, a 1925 Fokker that formed part of the Byrd Arctic expedition, and the very chair that Lincoln sat in when he was assassinated in 1865. The museum's highlight is, not surprisingly, noteworthy automobiles. Look for Henry Ford's 1901 Model-T, the Montgomery city bus in which Rosa Parks refused to give up her seat in 1955, and five presidential limos including the car in which Kennedy was assassinated in 1963. Adjacent to The Henry Ford is Greenfield Village, Ford's sprawling collection of historic homes, and the Ford Rouge Factory Tour featuring a walk-through of a Ford F-150 assembly plant.

20900 Oakwood Blvd., Dearborn 48124
313-982-6001
thehenryford.org

TIP
If you're interested in seeing multiple sections of The Henry Ford—the museum itself, Greenfield Village, and/or the Ford Rouge Factory Tour—buy a combination ticket for a substantial price savings on the second entrance fee.

WALK THROUGH AMERICAN HISTORY
AT GREENFIELD VILLAGE

If the Henry Ford Museum is America's attic, Greenfield Village is its back forty. The automotive giant's love of historic artifacts extended well beyond household objects to noteworthy houses and buildings, and it is at Greenfield Village that you can see his massive collection. Walk through Thomas Edison's Fort Meyers laboratory and his Menlo Park complex, where the scientist patented the electric lightbulb, the phonograph, and some four hundred other inventions. Visit the Wright Brothers's Dayton, Ohio, bicycle shop and the homes of poet Robert Frost and dictionary author Noah Webster. Colonial-era houses from Massachusetts, Connecticut, and New Hampshire are open to walk through as is a nineteenth-century Maryland plantation. There are even a Swiss chalet and a Cotswold cottage on-site, all of the properties purchased and subsequently moved here to Henry Ford's Dearborn property.

20900 Oakwood Blvd., Dearborn 48124
313-982-6001
thehenryford.org/village
Closed for the winter January through mid-April

SEE THE NATION'S FIRST AND ONLY
ARAB AMERICAN NATIONAL MUSEUM

Set in the heart of Detroit's largest Arab American community, Dearborn's Arab American National Museum focuses attention on the history and contributions of Arabs both here, in metro Detroit, and across the country. Archival photos, old passports, hand-knotted prayer rugs, even intricately drawn family trees recount the emigration of a people who trace their first appearance in North America to the sixteenth century. The Living in America gallery details how Arab Americans made their way in their adopted country through military records, peddlers' trunks, sewing machines, and other tools of the trades. But perhaps the most surprising part of the museum is the second floor gallery, Making an Impact. It's a sometimes surprising who's who of Arab Americans including Tony Shalhoub of the television series *Monk,* consumer advocate Ralph Nader, White House correspondent Helen Thomas, and schoolteacher/space shuttle astronaut Christa McAuliffe.

13624 Michigan Ave., Dearborn 48126
313-582-2266
arabamericanmuseum.org

UNDERSTAND THE AFRICAN AMERICAN EXPERIENCE
AT THE CHARLES H. WRIGHT MUSEUM OF AFRICAN AMERICAN HISTORY

Located beneath an impressive sixty-five-foot-high dome in Midtown Detroit's Cultural Center, the Charles Wright Museum houses over thirty-five thousand artifacts, making this the world's largest institution centered on the African American experience. Permanent exhibits explore the path of African Americans in this country, and visitors learn about the Underground Railroad (for which Detroit served as an endpoint), the Civil Rights movement, and the importance of African Americans in Detroit's powerful labor unions. Prominent African American success stories play an important role in the museum, and visitors will be inspired by the stories of scientist George Washington Carver, abolitionist Sojourner Truth, aviator Willa Brown Chappell, medical researcher Dr. Charles Richard Drew, and heavyweight boxer Joe Louis, who was himself a Detroiter.

315 E. Warren Ave., Detroit 48201
313-494-5800
thewright.org

SEE RUIN PORN RESTORED
AT THE BOOK CADILLAC HOTEL

When people talked about ruin porn, they were talking about places like the Book Cadillac Hotel. But that was then. Detroit's premier hotel is back in business, its ruins spectacularly restored as a Westin Hotel. At its 1924 opening on Washington Boulevard, dubbed the "Fifth Avenue of the Midwest," the Book Cadillac was the world's tallest hotel at thirty-three stories and functioned as a home away from home for celebrities and statesmen. The hotel shuttered its doors in the mid-1980s before falling horribly into disrepair by the early 2000s: ceilings collapsed, water pooled on the floor, saplings began to take root. In 2007 a major renovation effort was undertaken and the hotel reopened its doors in 2008, restored to its former grandeur with glittering chandeliers, shiny marble floors, and a design that melds the art deco with contemporary crispness.

1114 Washington Blvd., Detroit 48226
313-442-1600
bookcadillacwestin.com

> ### TIP
> When you check in, ask the front desk about a historic hotel tour or, if you prefer, a brochure about the historic property, "The Legend Returns."

EXPLORE ARCHITECTURAL TREASURES ON FOOT
WITH PRESERVATION DETROIT

Back in the 1920s, when Detroit was rolling in money, the city flaunted its success with grand architecture. There was the art deco Penobscot Building, the eighth-tallest building in the world when it was constructed in 1928. The Guardian Building, known as the "Cathedral of Finance" when it was built in 1929, was covered with nearly two million tangerine-colored bricks on the outside while its interior was decorated with gold leaf and tiled in a brightly colored Mayan design. The art deco, Albert Kahn-designed Fisher Building, also constructed in 1929, originally bore a gold-plated roof. These architectural gems and others find their place on tours with Preservation Detroit, an organization devoted to sharing the city's rich cultural heritage while using its profits to preserve even more Detroit buildings. Two-hour tours cover the highlights of three areas of Detroit: downtown, Midtown, or the Eastern Market.

313-577-3559
preservationdetroit.org

SEE THE NATION'S FIRST AUTO FACTORY,
THE FORD PIQUETTE AVENUE PLANT

You might say the Motor City was born on Piquette Avenue, where Henry Ford constructed his first automobile factory in 1904. Visitors can walk through this historic building to view painstakingly restored Model T's and the pre-assembly line work stations where they and twelve thousand others were built. The factory's backstory is detailed in a short film, which is followed by a visit to Piquette Avenue's automobile design center, the Experimental Room. Finally, visitors get a look at the office where America's automotive pioneer, Henry Ford, worked day in and day out. The Piquette Avenue Plant sits in the midst of the Piquette Avenue Industrial Historic District where Ford, Studebaker, Cadillac, Dodge, and supplier Fisher Body all had factories at one time. The district is largely abandoned now but once employed tens of thousands of automotive workers. The Ford Piquette Avenue Plant is open from April through Thanksgiving.

461 Piquette St., Detroit 48202
313-872-8759
fordpiquetteavenueplant.org

DISCOVER AFRICAN AMERICAN ART
AT THE N'NAMDI CENTER FOR CONTEMPORARY ART

This Midtown Detroit gallery was created by George N'Namdi, an art dealer with more than three decades of experience buying, selling, and collecting art. The center's large, bare, concrete interior forms the perfect neutral backdrop for its exhibits, many of them brilliant in color and size. Temporary works of national and international importance rotate with N'Namdi's permanent collection and works available for purchase: paintings and collages, sculpture, and textile works with a strong emphasis on contemporary African American artists. The center's permanent collection is considered one of the finest private collections of African American art in the world, with works by graphic artist and sculptor Elizabeth Catlett, tonalist painter Edward Mitchell Bannister, painter and sculptor Charles Searles, and Detroit native Allie McGhee, also a painter and sculptor.

52 E. Forest Ave., Detroit 48201
313-831-8700
nnamdicenter.org

CHECK OUT THE CARS OF TODAY AND TOMORROW
AT THE NORTH AMERICAN INTERNATIONAL AUTO SHOW

The world's latest and greatest vehicles—and a large number of concept cars—take the spotlight each January at the North American International Auto Show in Detroit's COBO Center. The NAIAS was launched way back in 1907 as a regional car show for the Detroit Area Dealer Association. What began more than a century ago with only seventeen cars has mushroomed in size, becoming one of the world's largest and most important auto events. Each year the NAIAS displays nearly eight hundred vehicles, from muscle cars to family sedans, from electric cars to heavy-duty full-size trucks. In addition to seeing the latest cars, visitors can learn about manufacturers' newest performance and environmental technology. Many of the automobiles on display have roots in Detroit's automotive industry. Others come from overseas, including Germany, Italy, Japan, and China, and several dozen of these receive their first-time worldwide introduction at the NAIAS.

naias.com

ATTEND A FESTIVAL
AT HART PLAZA

All of Detroit—and a fair number of visitors—meet at downtown's Hart Plaza. Set on the banks of the Detroit River, this is the site where it's believed Antoine de la Mothe Cadillac, the French explorer and founder of Detroit, first landed in 1701. Today Hart Plaza spans fourteen acres and can accommodate as many as forty thousand people for internationally recognized events like the Detroit Jazz Festival or the Movement Electronic Music Festival. A whole string of celebrations fills the plaza in summer, including the Detroit Fireworks. But Hart Plaza is also worth visiting sans the crowds. Check out its public art, including the circular steel Horace Dodge and Son Memorial Fountain, a statue of Cadillac, a memorial to the Underground Railroad, and several others. Along the park's northern edge, in the median of Woodward and Jefferson Avenues, is the famous *Monument to Joe Louis,* colloquially known as *The Fist,* an homage to the Detroit boxer.

1 Hart Plaza, Detroit 48226
313-877-8057
detroitmi.gov

CATCH
THE *SPIRIT OF DETROIT*

Detroiters's favorite statue—and they have a lot of statues to choose from—is the iconic bronze *Spirit of Detroit* in front of the Coleman A. Young Municipal Center downtown. Designed by Marshall Fredericks and dedicated in 1958, the twenty-six-foot-tall statue was the largest bronze monument cast anywhere in the world since the Renaissance. Fredericks never formally named the statue but Detroiters did, taking its name from the Bible verse inscribed behind it: "Now the Lord is that Spirit, and where the Spirit of the Lord is, there is liberty" (2 Corinthians 3:17). Most of the time the *Spirit of Detroit* sits unclothed, but Detroit's professional team jerseys—the Tigers, Lions, or Red Wings—occasionally adorn the bronze, particularly during the play-offs.

Woodward Ave. between E. Larned St. and Jefferson Ave.

TAKE THE BRIDGE (OR TUNNEL)
TO CANADA

The border crossing between Detroit and Windsor, Ontario, marks the busiest crossing between the United States and Canada. And while most of the traffic crossing this border is freight, citizens of both nations have been known to cross even for a few hours to take advantage of exchange rate bargains or to enjoy dinner with a new perspective out the restaurant window. Drive time from Michigan to Canada and back can vary widely depending on traffic and any security concerns of the moment. Travel either via the Detroit-Windsor Tunnel, which has allowed visitors to motor beneath the Detroit River since 1930, or via the steeply arching Ambassador Bridge for sweeping views of the Detroit River, the Detroit skyline, and America's neighbor to the north . . . although in actuality, Canada lies south of the US from Detroit. Don't forget your passport!

Detroit-Windsor Tunnel: E. Jefferson Ave. at Randolph St.
Ambassador Bridge: W. Jefferson Ave. at 21st St.

SHOOT A SELFIE
WITH THE GIANT UNIROYAL TIRE

A landmark in Detroit since 1965, the eighty-foot Uniroyal Tire was originally built as a tire-shaped Ferris wheel for the U.S. Rubber Pavilion at the 1964 New York World's Fair. More than two million visitors rode the wheel, including the Shah of Iran and First Lady Jacqueline Kennedy, while it operated at the fair. Afterward, the oversized tire was dismantled, the gap where the cars rotated was covered over with tread, and the whole thing was shipped to Uniroyal's offices in Detroit. Ever since, the giant Uniroyal's presence along I-94 in Allen Park has announced to the world their arrival in the Motor City. You can't go inside the tire these days as it sits on private property, but it's worth driving past this iconic Detroit landmark for a shot of the world's largest tire.

South side of I-94 just east of M-39 in Allen Park

JAM WITH KID ROCK AND HIS MOTOR CITY COMPADRES
AT THE DETROIT HISTORICAL MUSEUM

Everyone knows about Detroit's connection to the Motown sound. But there's a long and varied list of famous musicians who honed their musical chops in Detroit. The Kid Rock Music Lab at the Detroit Historical Museum includes the dizzying array of performers from Kid Rock himself to Bob Seger, Iggy Pop, Ted Nugent, Madonna, Anita Baker, Derrick May, Eminem, and the White Stripes, to name just a few. Naturally, the DHM includes plenty of exhibits about Detroit's nonmusical history too. Follow the city's progression from frontier town to industrial hub in the Detroiters at Work gallery; learn about the city's role as leading manufacturer of World War II tanks and fighter planes in Arsenal of Democracy; and see a recreated automobile assembly line in America's Motor City.

5401 Woodward Ave., Detroit 48202
313-833-1805
detroithistorical.org

VISIT SAARINEN'S HOUSE
AT THE CRANBROOK ART MUSEUM

One of the nation's preeminent art and science institutes, Cranbrook embodied the best of the arts and crafts movement at the turn of the twentieth century. The school joined together the architectural and creative genius of Eliel and son Eero Saarinen, Albert Kahn, Carl Milles, Marshall Fredericks, and Charles and Ray Eames, all of them teaching, studying, and designing functional artworks guided by the idea of enlightening a burgeoning middle class. Cranbrook's Art Museum is worth a visit, with exhibits of works that range from these design innovators to works produced by the institute's current student body. Take time to explore Cranbrook's grounds, which are just as intriguing, with stops at the art deco house built and occupied by Eliel Saarinen, one of Cranbrook's founders and an early school educator, and the Smith House, designed by Frank Lloyd Wright.

39221 Woodward Ave., Bloomfield Hills 48303
248-645-3323
cranbrookart.edu

TIP
Cranbrook's Art Museum is open year-round and includes access to the institute's sizable and impressive sculpture garden. House tours are limited from May to October. Reservations are required.

DISCOVER PUBLIC ART
AT THE STATIONS
OF THE PEOPLE MOVER

Until Detroit unveils its new M-1 light rail line in 2017, the best public transit in downtown Detroit is the People Mover. The elevated monorail system forms a three-mile loop making stops at destinations like the COBO Center, Joe Louis Arena, and Greektown. Take note of the art within each of the People Mover's thirteen stations. Fifteen artists (nine of them from Michigan) were selected to create these site-specific works, many of them constructed of Detroit-made Pewabic tiles. Favorites include The *Blue Nile,* a rendition of an African Noah's Ark by Charles McGee at the Broadway station; *Catching Up,* the realistic statue of a man reading a newspaper by J. Seward Johnson Jr. at Grand Circus Park; and *Cavalcade of Cars,* a large mural of seven vintage automobiles by Larry Ebel and Linda Cianciolo Scarlett at the COBO Center stop.

thepeoplemover.com

OVERNIGHT
AT GM HEADQUARTERS, THE RENAISSANCE CENTER

General Motors's Renaissance Center ranks as the most recognizable landmark in Detroit's city skyline. Constructed in 1977, the cluster of six round glass-and-steel skyscrapers that makes up the "RenCen," as Detroiters call it, includes so much real estate that the building has its own zip code. GM claims much of the space—this is their world headquarters, after all—but there's much more to see and do. A wonderful full-service Marriott hotel occupies much of the building's center tower. The fine dining restaurant Coach Insignia sits at the very top of the building, while in the RenCen's lower level you'll find a display of GM's current automotive offerings as well as an inexpensive food court. Several shops and restaurants fill the remaining space, including the glass Winter Garden, which houses still more shopping and dining and provides access to the Detroit Riverwalk.

100 Renaissance Center, Detroit 48243
313-567-3126
gmrencen.com

TIP
Interested in seeing more of the Renaissance Center?
Take a free one-hour tour of the building offered every weekday.

SET YOUR HAIR ON END
AT THE MICHIGAN SCIENCE CENTER

Shrieks of laughter—and a lot of static electricity—fill the air at the Sparks Electricity Show, standing participants' hair on end and introducing kids to the cool side of science experiments. The thirty-minute show is one of several adult-guided, hands-on educational sessions at Midtown Detroit's interactive science center. Other topics include science labs that demonstrate the power of air pressure, the variations in chemical reactions, and the possibilities of new technology. The Michigan Science Center also houses a planetarium, a simulated road construction center, and a program-it-yourself robotics lab where science and art overlap. The exhibits are aimed at exciting young people about the fields of science, technology, and math, subjects of great importance in an engineering hub like Detroit. But the Michigan Science Center also succeeds in making those subjects wildly fun.

5020 John R St., Detroit 48202
313-577-8400
mi-sci.org

SEE HOW THE OTHER HALF LIVED
AT THE EDSEL FORD HOUSE

Henry Ford's only son, Edsel, and his wife, Eleanor, weren't hurting for money when they commissioned the construction of this 1926 home in tony Grosse Pointe Shores. One of Detroit's most elegant historic homes, the brick English Tudor estate was designed by noted architect Albert Kahn to resemble a Cotswold cottage. Eighty-six grassy, wooded acres surround the estate on three sides, the fourth splashed by the lovely waters of Lake St. Clair. Outside, the estate's stone walls and roof are adorned with lead glass windows and climbing ivy. Inside, the thirty-thousand-square-foot house is furnished just as it was when the Fords lived and raised their family here. Sixteenth-century English wood paneling and heavy stone fireplaces were salvaged in Europe and transported to the Fords's home here, giving the house the appearance that it is much older than it is. Look for original Cézannes and Diego Riveras on the walls.

1100 Lakeshore Rd., Grosse Pointe Shores 48236
313-884-4222
fordhouse.org

SHOPPING AND FASHION

BUY A DETROIT-MADE WATCH
AT SHINOLA

When Tom Kartsotis, founding member of Fossil, decided to launch a manufacturing company dedicated to producing quality American-made watches, he looked to Detroit. This was, after all, a city where quality manufacturing had been a way of life for over a century, a place where knowing how to make things lies in the DNA. Manufactured using watch movements from Switzerland, Shinolas's inner workings and their remaining components are assembled by Detroiters in a former automotive research lab in Midtown's Taubman Building. You can take a free tour of Shinola's assembly area, a pristine work station where employees wear hairnets and lab coats, or shop at the luxury watchmaker's flagship store, also in Midtown. Although Shinola is known for its timepieces, the company also manufactures high-end bicycles and leather goods.

Shinola Tour: 485 W. Milwaukee St., Detroit 48202
844-744-6652

Flagship Store: 441 W. Canfield St., Detroit 48201
313-285-2390

shinola.com

BROWSE HANDCRAFTED CERAMICS
AT PEWABIC POTTERY

Founded in Detroit in 1903 during the height of the arts and crafts movement, Pewabic found immense success handcrafting architectural tiles. Mary Chase Perry Stratton was the brains behind the business from the very start, experimenting with various ceramic glazes until she settled on an iridescent glaze that brought the potter national acclaim. Pewabic tiles were considered among the most innovative of their time by the second decade of the twentieth century and were sought after across the country. In Detroit, you can see tangerine-colored Pewabic tiles on the exterior of the Guardian Building and in many People Mover stations. Elsewhere, the ceramic tiles grace Chicago's Shedd Aquarium and the Nebraska State Capitol, and they're part of the collections at the DIA, Washington's Freer Gallery, and the Louvre in Paris. Buy your own ceramic pieces—decorative tiles, handcrafted mugs and bowls, and holiday ornaments—at Pewabic's workshop just east of downtown.

10125 E. Jefferson Ave., Detroit 48214
313-626-2000
pewabic.org

SHOW YOUR LOVE FOR THE D
AT PURE DETROIT

In 1998 Pure Detroit began an effort at revitalizing the city by investing in locally owned retail shops and cafes. In the more than fifteen years since, the organization has blossomed to include retail stores in three of Detroit's architectural gems — the GM Renaissance Center, the Guardian Building, and the Fisher Building—promoting and selling food, clothing, gifts, and accessories made in the Motor City. Some of the items on sale at Pure Detroit—locally roasted coffee beans, Pewabic art tiles, and handmade coasters— are produced within the city, generating income for Detroit's homegrown entrepreneurs. Other items fall into the realm of civic cheerleading: T-shirts silkscreened with iconic Detroit automotive logos, belts and handbags constructed of seatbelts, and necklaces that incorporate bits of old Detroit city maps.

Guardian Building Lobby, 500 Griswold, Suite 250, Detroit 48226
313-963-1440

Fisher Building Lobby, 3011 W. Grand Blvd., Suite 101, Detroit 48202
313-873-7873

GM Renaissance Center, Tower 400, Detroit 48243
313-259-5100

puredetroit.com

DRESS FOR SUCCESS
AT JOHN VARVATOS

An accomplished luxury menswear designer whose résumé includes heading up the men's fashion divisions at such impressive houses as Polo Ralph Lauren and Calvin Klein, John Varvatos launched his own fashion house in 1999 and soon after starred in the NBC reality show *Fashion Star*. Varvatos, who was born and raised in Detroit, melds subtle rock 'n' roll and industrial influences into his upscale clothing and accessories lines, including leather biker jackets, boots, and studded belts. John Varvatos retail stores are located all around the world, from Bangkok to New York, from London to Mexico City. But since the fashion guru is a native Detroiter, you may as well visit his store in downtown Detroit, just off Grand Circus Park. Shop for jackets, jeans, shoes, belts, and attachés.

1500 Woodward Ave., Detroit 48226
313-437-8095
johnvarvatos.com

DISCOVER INDEPENDENT BOUTIQUES
AT REVITALIZED MIDTOWN

There are few places where Detroit's comeback is more visible than in Midtown. Centered on Woodward Avenue and stretching from West Grand Boulevard in the north to the area around Grand Circus Park to the south, Midtown was just a few years ago pocked with derelict buildings and empty lots save for the museums of the Cultural District. These days Midtown is hopping with young creative types, its storefronts reimagined as independent boutiques or dining spaces. And those that remain empty? They're most likely under renovation by the next new entrepreneur. Expect the addition of the city's new light rail, the M-1, to make Midtown even busier in years to come. Most of Midtown's shopping sits near Cass Avenue at Canfield with other hot spots at the Park Shelton Building on Woodward and near the Fisher Building on West Grand Boulevard.

The Black Dress Co.
Women's clothing and accessories
87 E. Canfield St., Detroit 48201
313-833-7795

Cass Corridog
Toys, clothing, care products,
and treats for dogs and cats
34240 Cass Ave., #110, Detroit 48201
313-887-9684
casscorridog.com

City Bird
Home decor, kitchen goods, apparel, and accessories
created by independent artists and designers from
Detroit and other Rust Belt cities
460 W. Canfield St., Detroit 48201
313-831-9146
ilovecitybird.com

Vera Jane
Handbags, fine lingerie, vintage jewelry,
and music by female recording artists
Fisher Building Lobby, 3011 W. Grand Blvd., Detroit
48202
313-875-4588

Workshop
Modern furniture crafted from reclaimed
Detroit building materials
Fisher Building Lobby, 3011 W. Grand Blvd., Detroit
48202
248-906-5926
workshopdetroit.com

BROWSE THE SHOPS
AT MIDTOWN'S PARK SHELTON BUILDING

Set just north of the Detroit Institute of Arts and the superb institutions of the Cultural District, the Park Shelton Building boasts a spot in the middle of the up-and-coming Midtown neighborhood. This block of Woodward Avenue benefited from its location near the city's best museums. But the dinginess of the surrounding city streets hurt business until recently, when various public-private partnerships began bringing in investment money. Midtown is immensely popular these days, bursting with new start-ups and anxious for the completion of a new light rail line that promises even more traffic. The Park Shelton Building has been fully restored to house luxury condominiums. But the building's ground floor houses several fun retail shops and a couple of casual restaurants as well.

15 E. Kirby St., Detroit 48202
313-872-PARK
theparkshelton.com

Busted Bra Shop
Specialty lingerie shop stocking
a huge variety of colors, styles, and sizes
313-288-0449
bustedindetroit.com

Frida and the Peacock Room
Companion shops to one another, both boutiques
specialize in unique and fun women's clothing and
accessories with Frida leaning toward casual wear and
the Peacock Room a bit fancier.
313-559-5500
facebook.com/fridadetroit
facebook.com/peacockroom

CHECK OUT SOME HARDCORE PAWN
AT AMERICAN JEWELRY & LOAN

Viewers of the wildly popular TruTV series *Hardcore Pawn* enjoy the opportunity to see the shop where pawnbroker Les Gold and his kids Seth and Ashley make their deals. Les made his first sale at the age of seven working in his father's pawn shop, Sam's Loan. As his own businessman, Les launched American Jewelry & Loan, which has been bargaining with Detroit residents since 1978. Now AJL ranks as the largest pawn shop in Detroit, making loans out of a fifty-thousand-square-foot downtown facility and operating a branch store in the northern suburb of Pontiac. The Gold family still likes to think of AJL as the place "where Detroit cashes in," welcoming shoppers to an inventory of sixty-eight thousand items. See the shop that made AJL famous . . . and with any luck, head home with a bargain-priced fur coat, jewelry, power tools, or electronics equipment.

Original shop: 20450 Greenfield, Detroit 48235
313-345-4000

Branch: 29 S. Telegraph Rd., Pontiac 48341
248-409-5626

pawndetroit.com

SUPPORT LOCAL ARTISTS
AT THE DETROIT ARTISTS MARKET

This Midtown Detroit market has been promoting the city's art community since 1932, both those artists who are well established and those whose talents are just emerging. Begun in the midst of the Great Depression as a means of helping struggling artists support themselves, the DAM originally focused on giving a hand up to artists under the age of thirty. But for many years now artists of all ages have been exhibiting and selling some of Detroit's best contemporary works from its Woodward Avenue storefront. The shopping is good here year-round, but you'll find an expanded selection of gift-worthy pieces around the holidays. Look for works of all types—sculpture, painting, photography, jewelry, ceramics, even original greeting cards and buttons—at a wide range of price points.

4719 Woodward Ave., Detroit 48201
313-832-8540
detroitartistsmarket.org

FIND ARTY GIFTS
AT THE DETROIT INSTITUTE OF ARTS

As is the case at most art museums, the DIA's gift shop offers beautiful hardcover books, DVDs, toys, and wearable art pieces related to the temporary exhibit of the moment. But the DIA's superb collection of African American art and its Diego Rivera *Detroit Industry* murals translate into a nice selection of souvenirs, home decor, and gifts related to these subjects: *The Detroit Industry Murals Fold-Out Book,* African American art books, Mali wedding glass bead necklaces, and even Diego Rivera finger puppets and Frida Kahlo paper dolls. You'll also find some nice Detroit-centric gifts, including books about Detroit ruin porn; books about Detroit's ongoing revitalization and the city's public art; handbags and belts made from seatbelt material; and decorative tiles, trivets, and paperweights made by Detroit-based pottery house Pewabic.

5200 Woodward Ave., Detroit 48202
313-833-7900
dia.org

"YOU BETTER SHOP AROUND. . ."
AT THE MOTOWN MUSEUM

When Berry Gordy launched the Motown music label at his studio on Detroit's West Grand Boulevard, he simultaneously launched the careers of dozens of American music icons, many of them Detroiters. The heart and soul of the Motown sound remains at Detroit's Hitsville U.S.A, the Motown Museum, as does the music of its legendary artists: Smokey Robinson, Diana Ross and the Supremes, Martha and the Vandellas, the Four Tops, Rare Earth, Stevie Wonder, Gladys Knight, and many others. Pick up a collection of quintessential music on CD or DVD at the Motown Museum gift store, recordings that range from the Miracles's *Shop Around,* Motown's first million-copy seller, to DVDs of *Lady Sings the Blues,* a Motown flick about Billie Holiday featuring the label's own Diana Ross.

2648 W. Grand Blvd., Detroit 48208
313-875-2264
motownmuseum.org

STOCK UP ON VINYL
AT THIRD MAN RECORDS

Although Third Man was launched in 2009, it wasn't until late 2015 that the company unveiled a Detroit location, its second following a Nashville opening in 2009. The brainchild of Jack White of White Stripes fame, Third Man's location on Midtown's Canfield Street represents something of a return to White's roots. The Detroit-born singer, songwriter, and record producer staged the White Stripes's first concert in 1997 just blocks away on Cass Avenue. Third Man Records sells music recordings, vinyl, and other Third Man merch. But a vinyl pressing operation, one of only a couple dozen in the US, opened in early 2016 making this shop even more interesting to visit. Customers can watch vinyl recordings produced behind a glass wall, then make their way to the cash register to buy them.

441 W. Canfield St., Detroit 48201
313-209-5205
thirdmanrecords.com

COVER YOUR HEAD
AT HENRY THE HATTER

They say it was Dwight Eisenhower's decision to wear one of Henry's hats at his 1953 presidential inauguration that put Henry the Hatter on the map. But Detroit's premier hatmaker had been producing quality caps long before anyone had heard of Ike. Since 1893 Henry the Hatter has been helping patrons select hats to fit their personality, physical characteristics, and wardrobe styles. The hatmaker's shop on Broadway has a humble appearance, with neon red letters glowing above simple plate-glass windows. But the shop has established itself as one of the nation's finest milliners, selling bowlers, fedoras, porkpies, even berets and aviator caps. Such celebrities as Kid Rock, comedian Steve Harvey, and Detroit luxury menswear designer John Varvatos are regular customers at Henry the Hatter.

1307 Broadway St., Detroit 48226
313-962-0970

15616 W. 10 Mile Rd., Southfield 48075
248-557-7770

henrythehatterdetroit.com

GIVE YOUR SPORTS TEAMS SOME LOVE
AT DETROIT ATHLETIC CO.

Love the Lions? Have a thing for the Tigers or the Red Wings? You'll find jerseys and caps, neckties and earrings, autographed baseball cards, souvenir programs . . . really, if it's got anything to do with Detroit's pro sports teams, you'll find it at the Detroit Athletic Co. The athletic clothing store sits in Detroit's thriving Corktown neighborhood, a community that saw a lot of foot traffic thirty years ago thanks to the location of Tiger Stadium at Michigan and Trumbull. In fact, the owners of the Detroit Athletic Co. got their start as kids hawking peanuts to Tigers fans. The Tigers moved to downtown Comerica Park in 2000, sending the Corktown neighborhood into a bit of a tailspin. But the community has been on the upswing in the past decade, drawing numerous locals and tourists to independent shops like this one. You can still see the old field today, now converted into a community and youth baseball diamond.

1744 Michigan Ave., Detroit 48216
877-604-4490
detroitathletic.com

RELEASE YOUR INNER BOOKWORM
AT JOHN K. KING USED & RARE BOOKS

Science fiction and graphic novels, mythology and home improvement, picture books and poetry and classics. Used books of every imaginable genre fill the towering shelves at John K. King. The four-story building looks from the outside as if it's seen better days. In fact, it used to be the Advance Glove factory, a manufacturer of industrial work gloves for metro Detroit. But inside is a treasure trove of books, all carefully alphabetized by author. You'll find a floor plan of the massive building and its large collection near the checkout at the entrance. Pick one up to narrow your search for a particular title. If you're still having difficulty laying your hand on just the right book, ask one of the friendly staff members, each wearing a red apron.

901 W. Lafayette Blvd., Detroit 48226
313-961-0622
kingbooksdetroit.com

BROWSE VINTAGE GEMS
AT ELDORADO GENERAL STORE

Maybe it was destined to be that Detroit's coolest vintage store would set up shop in Corktown, the oldest surviving neighborhood in the city. "Well-curated vintage" is how owner Erin Gavle describes the inventory at Eldorado, a shop set in the heart of a newly revitalized community. Surrounded by exposed brick walls and well-worn wooden floors are displays of Erin's hand-picked clothing, accessories, and decor, displays so attractive you wonder if they were meant to be photographed. Eldorado's products run the gamut, from buttery-soft, fringed suede jackets to sequined handbags, from jaunty fedoras to appliquéd cowboy boots, silver tea sets, and bouquets of dried flowers. Pre-loved items all bear a little tag highlighting where they were discovered: Brooklyn, New York; Austin, Texas; Portland, Maine.

1700 Michigan Ave., Detroit 48216
734-664-8633
eldoradogeneralstore.com

SHOP THE EDGES
OF EASTERN MARKET

Detroit's Eastern Market is best known for the six sheds that sell produce and flowers, baked goods, and preserves in a designated four-and-a-half-acre district north of downtown. Since 1841 everyone from grandmothers to high-end chefs have headed to these downtown city blocks for fresh ingredients. But alongside the sheds of locally grown veggies and cut flowers are streets lined with independently owned shops, dozens of retailers selling these very same items, if on a smaller scale. You'll also find Detroit-made food products that are more processed than your standard farmers market fare: locally made pop, snack foods, chocolates, and beer. Besides food items, look for home decor and salvaged industrial items, original art, and T-shirts singing the praises of The D. Eastern Market is rimmed by Rivard, Wilkins, and Orleans Streets and East Fisher Service Dr.

Aria Urban Artifacts
Antique furniture, housewares, and art
2463 Riopelle St., Detroit 48207
313-365-0411

Detroit Mercantile Co.
Locally made products from
Carhartt jackets to Faygo pop, Better Made chips,
and Detroit musicians on vinyl
3434 Russell St., Detroit 48207
313-831-9000
detroitmercantile.com

Germack
House-roasted nuts, seeds, and coffee beans
2517 Russell St., Detroit 48207
313-784-9484
germack.com

Michigan Artisans
Jewelry, handbags, scarves, books, and music
all created by artists from the state of Michigan
1400 E. Fisher Service Dr., Detroit 48207
313-355-4316
michigan-artisans.org

SEARCH FOR HIGH-END FINDS
IN SMALL-TOWN BIRMINGHAM

This affluent suburb in northwest Detroit combines the best aspects of a small town with those of a well-to-do urban neighborhood. The community truly is small. Some twenty thousand residents live in a town that covers fewer than five square miles. But Birmingham's location between downtown Detroit and the northern suburb of Pontiac, its proximity to several wealthy suburbs, and its focus on a pedestrian-friendly downtown and upscale retail shops and services have made the town a popular place to spend some money. Nearly three hundred downtown Birmingham shops sell items ranging from precious and costume jewelry to fashion, antiques, and art. Urban bike paths, fine dining, salons, day spas, and more than twenty parks make Birmingham a nice place to spend a day outside of the big city.

enjoybirmingham.com

ArtLoft
Handcrafted watches and clocks, artisan jewelry,
ceramic and textile art pieces
123 W. Maple Rd.
248-647-4007
artloftonline.com

Barbara Boz Boutique
Designer jewelry and accessories
205 E. Maple Rd.
248-310-0978
barbarabozboutique.com

Nina McLemore
Designer clothing for executive women
550 W. Merrill St., Suite 230
248-430-4365
ninamclemore.com

The Sports Gallery
Sports, entertainment, historical
and political memorabilia
255 E. Brown St.
248-642-0044
sports-gallery.com

DRESS YOURSELF IN NAVY AND ORANGE
AT THE D SHOP AT COMERICA PARK

Team jerseys and baseball caps, MLB memorabilia, and navy and orange onesies, Tigers fans find thousands of ways to show support for their team at the D Shop. Comerica Park brought the Tigers to the heart of the city in 2000, when the team abandoned their former home at Corktown's Tigers Stadium for a more modern, centrally located stadium downtown. The Woodward Avenue location makes it easier for baseball fans to enjoy Detroit's city attractions on game day. Comerica also makes it easier for downtown visitors to get their game on year-round. Located on the northwest corner of Comerica Park, the store opens onto the street as well as the stadium, so fans can shop even when the Tigers aren't scheduled to play at home.

2100 Woodward Ave., Detroit 48201
313-471-2673
detroit.tigers.mlb.com/det/ballpark

BUY DESIGNER GOODS
AT THE SOMERSET COLLECTION

Located in Detroit's northwest suburbs, the Somerset Collection ranks as metro Detroit's premier shopping mall—and one of its largest. Two massive buildings are joined into one by means of a glass skyway that straddles Troy's Big Beaver Road. The mall wings themselves are spacious and airy, brightened with glass atria. High-end, name-brand shopping is the watchword at this exclusive shopping mall. Look for Giorgio Armani and Hervé Leger, kate spade, Omega watches, Saks Fifth Avenue, and Gucci, all with storefronts at the Somerset Collection. Quality service is customary at Somerset too, including the services of a shopping concierge. If money is a wee bit tighter than that, you'll find more mainstream stores as well such as Macy's, Pottery Barn, and Williams-Sonoma.

2800 W. Big Beaver Rd., Troy 48084
248-643-6360
thesomersetcollection.com

TIP
Need help with transportation? The Somerset Collection offers valet parking and complimentary use of wheelchairs and strollers. Call ahead if you'd like complimentary use of a motorized scooter.

DISCOVER A FLASH FROM THE PAST
AT THE DETROIT SHOPPE

Located within the Somerset Collection shopping mall, the Detroit Shoppe, like so many up-and-coming Detroit retailers, capitalizes on the pride of The D by selling Detroit-centric products. Better Made snacks, Faygo pop, Detroit sports memorabilia, and Pewabic pottery tiles all find a place on this store's shelves. The Detroit Shoppe also amasses a selection of gifts from the city's cultural institutions: recorded Motown music, arty gifts from the Detroit Institute of Arts, and history books published by the Wright Museum of African American History. Between and behind store shelves is an assortment of historical items, giving the shop something of a museum quality. Seats from the old Tiger Stadium, historic photos, and posters of Detroit's biggest music acts make the Detroit Shoppe worth a visit even if you're not certain you want to buy.

2800 W. Big Beaver Rd., Troy 48084
248-816-5470
thedetroitshoppe.com

SUGGESTED
ITINERARIES

AFRICAN AMERICAN HERITAGE

AUTOMOTIVE HERITAGE

CLASSIC DETROIT

COMEBACK CITY

MUSIC

WITH THE FAMILY

Detroit Water Ice Factory, 17
Detroit Zoo, 57
Eastern Market, 123
Garden Bowl, 35
Giant Uniroyal Tire, 94
Greenfield Village, 83
Henry Ford Museum, 82
Michigan Science Center, 100
Outdoor Adventure Center, 63
People Mover, 97
Sanders Chocolates, 9
Sea Life Michigan Aquarium, 76
Westview Orchards, 31
Wheelhouse Detroit, 62

SPORTS-LOVER

Belle Isle, 61
Comerica Park, 59
Corner Tap Room, 20
Detroit Athletic Co., 120
Elwood Bar & Grill, 27
Ford Field, 66
Grand Trunk Pub, 28
Hockeytown Cafe, 24
Joe Louis Arena, 56
Palace of Auburn Hills, 53
The D Shop at Comerica Park, 128
Tiger Stadium Field, 67

DATE NIGHT

ACTIVITIES
BY SEASON

INDEX